The Modular

David Warwick

Basil Blackwell

First published 1987
© David Warwick 1987

Published by Basil Blackwell Ltd
108 Cowley Road
Oxford OX4 1JF
England

British Library Cataloguing in Publication Data

Warwick, David
The modular curriculum.
  1. Curriculum planning – Great Britain
  I. Title
  375'.001'0941   LB1564.G7

ISBN 0-631-15324-1

Typeset in 10pt Sabon
by MULTIPLEX techniques ltd, St Mary Cray, Kent.
Printed in Great Britain
at T.J. Press (Padstow) Ltd., Cornwall

Contents

Case Studies

Curricular Items

1   External Accreditation of Modules, Northern Partnership for Records of Achievement
2   Modular taster units, TVEI
3   *Setting out the store* from Yorkshire Television's *Be Your Own Boss*
4   Core modules in music, Southern Regional Examination Board
5   Modular pathways, Ysgol Emrys ap Iwan
6   Flexible modules, CPVE
7   Modular choice within the Open University
8   The 'core' of 'A' level economics
9   Managerial training through modules, Thorn EMI
10   Complementary modules, Middleton Park High School, Leeds
11   Chronological sequence, Peers School, Oxford
12   *Modular signposting*, Buckinghamshire College of Higher Education
13   Optional units, Northern Examining Association GCSE Science
14   Compulsory Core Module, 'A' level Art and Design, Cambridgeshire, TVEI Consortium
15   Banked module from pastoral curriculum, Farnham College, Surrey
16   Industrial model for specification
17   Strong and weak objectives
18   Preparing a unit for accreditation, Hemsworth High School, Yorkshire
19   Learning strategies, S W Region Curriculum Base
20   Submission of modules, Northern Partnership for Records of Achievement
21   Proforma for submission of 'A' level units, Cambridgeshire TVEI Consortium
22   Modular specification, Northern Ireland Council for Educational Development
23   *Getting the Message Across* Hemsworth High School, Yorkshire
24   Facilitating modular choice and balance, Ysgol Emrys ap Iwan
25   Module within stratified scheme, Thomas Tallis School, London
26   Free-standing and open module, Ysgol Emrys ap Iwan
27   Free-standing module written in behavioural terms, Peers School, Oxford
28   Modular specification for student choice, Parliament Hill School, London

Introduction

Few curricular innovations can have received such widespread attention than has the approach through modules, which seems to have equal appeal for teachers, pupils and students in every sector of the educational system.

Such planning can currently be found operating successfully at every level: in infant, primary, middle and secondary schools; colleges of further and higher education; universities; and within schemes of managerial training in commerce and in industry. Some of the newer examinations – CPVE and BTEC, for example – incorporate the modular approach as a basic element, whilst many schools are beginning to find that GCSE may be tackled with greater rationality and increased cross-curricular coherence along such lines. TVEI, Open Tech, and YTS programmes have all experimented successfully with modules, and they are fundamental to the work of distance-learning agencies such as the National Extension College and the Open University. Furthermore, modular planning has found its way into every aspect of school or college life. Here, the academic, pastoral, vocational and social dimensions can all be cited.

From this it might seem that the curricular millenium has arrived – that the meagre module should now be written about in terms approaching that of the Holy Grail. Such, however, is far from the truth. There is a serious fallacy underlying any campaign to elevate it to such a lofty position; to regard the approach as a panacea for all educational ills. The fact of the matter is that modular planning is not a theory in its own right. It does not follow that if you have seen one modular scheme you have seen them all, as the many examples given in the pages that follow testify. To claim that one works through modules is the equivalent of confiding that one's wife is pretty, that a film is boring, that a pupil is clever or that a piece of string is long. Such information is in itself meaningless unless placed in context and considered with reference to wider criteria.

The term *module*, then, has little meaning on its own. It is the way in which such units are *used* that is important, and it is from the aims of those utilising them that they derive their significance. From this apparent weakness stems the modules' strength. They are enormously adaptive, and may be put to use in a myriad ways – often by those who in ideology and practice are poles apart. The traditionalist seeks to give direction to his work by breaking down its content into cognitivitely meaningful sections. The progressive permits pupils to construct their own curriculum from a large number of free-standing, independent modules. The behaviouralist shapes the learning process by a gradual progression through carefully-sequenced units, rewarding success with a series of credits, whilst the devotee of experiential work looks to modules to rescue creativity from the tyranny of the timetable. Each extracts exactly what he requires, emphasising those aspects of modular planning which best suit the work in hand or developments which are to be fostered. Modules are not ends in themselves. Rather, chameleon-like, they can be made to take on the colouration of the curricular patterns that surround them.

The dangers, as well as the advantages, of such eclecticism should be obvious. Modules cannot easily be transferred bodily from one context to another without the risk of tissue rejection. If the aims of each institution are identical, the transplant may work: if not, modules are as likely to fragment a curriculum as they are to develop it; they may bring discontinuity and discord in their wake. It is not therefore surprising that the approach succeeds in institutions where there is a clear rationale for what is done, but tends to fail where an appeal to some amorphous 'modular planning' seeks to paper over such a void. Modules are excellent servants, but anarchic masters.

This book sets out to assist schools, colleges or consortia considering the introduction of planning through modules, or already experimenting with such an approach. It does so by attempting to clarify the issues involved and suggesting how their work can be strengthened and enriched through this approach. No one way is favoured above others; rather the line taken is that methodology must follow aims and that once decisions regarding the direction and balance of the work have been made, modules can be used to enhance and to support them. These stages are set out in a fairly logical fashion. Readers with experience of modular planning may wish to turn directly to specific chapters, but those new to the approach are recommended to read them in sequence.

The first chapter sets out the case for modules, bringing together the many and varied benefits that can accrue from their introduction. In Chapter Two the various theoretical justifications for such planning are brought together and presented as a basic model – *The Modular Transverse* – which is referred to throughout the rest of the book. Chapters Three and Four describe how modules can be used at various levels throughout the system, from infant school through to higher education, and Chapter Five gives an overview of the different ways in which modules may be combined to translate aims into practice.

The next two chapters (Six and Seven) concentrate on the planning and preparation of modules, together with their presentation to pupils, students, parents and employers, whilst Chapter Eight deals specifically with approaches of a highly participative or experiential nature at all levels. Running through the book there is an emphasis upon formative assessment, contractual relationships, the building up of records of achievement or profiles and the personal guidance of students in their modular choices. These are dealt with in more detail in the final two chapters (Nine and Ten).

Inevitably, when covering such a wide variation of age, experience and content, the book has had to be written in fairly general terms. It does not, for example, set out to instruct how a fourth year module on Pollution, presented in an all-girls school at Ross-on-Wye should be tackled! Rather, it aims to offer teachers all the information they require to make the planning, teaching and evaluation of such a unit possible. Indeed, it would be mistaken for any writer to believe that he knows more about the actual needs and conditions of specific classes than do those who meet them on a day-to-day basis. To overcome this problem of generality, I have made full use of first-hand examples taken from a wide range of schools and colleges. The *case-studies* describe the way in which whole schools, or large sections of them, operate: the *curricular items* are short, more direct and deal with specific issues. I would like to express my gratitude to all the institutions which most generously allowed me to make use of their work in this way.

A second problem involved terminology. What should I call the recipients of all this planning? Are they 'children', 'pupils' or 'students'? Reflecting once more the versatility of modular approaches, each term is appropriate at certain points within the text, inappropriate at others. I have tried to resolve this issue by using 'pupil' as far as possible for those up to the age of 14, and 'student' beyond this age.

There is also the dilemma of what to do about gender. The book began life peppered with 'he/she', 'him/her', 'his/hers', '(s)he', etc. Although technically accurate and diplomatically sound, I personally found this to be stylistically awkward and felt that it gave an untidy appearance to the page. Readers (and especially my friend who serves 'Ploughpersons' Lunches' in the public house outside Midhurst!) should read 'her' for 'him', 'she' for 'he', etc, throughout the text, as appropriate.

The *For further reading* sections at the conclusion of each chapter are designed for those who wish to follow up the ideas traced in each, although not necessarily within the confines of modular planning: the final *Index* should take readers directly to the part of the text they require.

David Warwick
Farnham, November 1986

1 Why modules?

The term *module* is usually taken to mean a single unit, complete in itself, but which may be added to further units towards the achievement of a larger task or a more long-term goal.

Sometimes individual need or *choice* is the guiding principle behind such planning. Modular kitchens, to take a fairly commonplace example, consist of a variety of units, each fulfilling a specialist function – cooking, breakfasting, storage, dishwashing, refrigeration etc. Rather than accepting a ready-made design, it is possible to select just the units which are required, or which can be afforded, and to have the freedom of setting these out according to the family's taste. Additional modules may then be added at a later date.

Other modular schemes depend not on choice for their success, but the *order* in which each unit is selected. This will be determined by the overall problem that has to be solved. A good example may be cited from the field of space exploration. Rockets are designed as a series of modules, each of which has a specific purpose. But they have to be fired at precisely the right moment and are jettisoned when their particular function has been performed. The task itself determines the *sequence* of units; to permit even a modicum of choice would jeopardise the entire enterprise.

A third use of modules relates neither to choice nor sequence. Rather, it is the *internal relationship* of the individual modules which takes precedence. In the completion of a jigsaw puzzle, for example, there can be no debate over the shape or the look of the finished product. This is dictated entirely by the picture or pattern that one is attempting to reconstruct. Nor is the sequence in which individual modules (the pieces) are selected of any great importance. It is possible to begin with all those having straight edges in order to construct the frame; to commence with all the pieces of one colour; or even to start with separate identifiable shapes within the whole. It is the relationship of individual modules one to the other and how they combine to make up the total 'picture' which is the determining factor throughout.

Curricular modules

The modular approach has for some time been applied at various levels within our educational system. Pioneering work was done in higher and further education. Modular planning has also been introduced with great success into industrial training courses, and the approach is now beginning to find its way into schools.

The pattern throughout is once more that of the presentation of material as a series of small units which may then be combined one with another in a variety of ways. The actual mechanics of the process will differ according to the age of the pupils and the nature of the work, but the rationale remains very much that already outlined. Some schemes are introduced to provide greater freedom of choice for those tackling them; others utilise modules either as sequential stepping-stones to a greater understanding of the subject-matter or as individual links which bind together hitherto separate areas of academic enquiry.

The advantages of such an approach within the educational context, then, can be found in three closely interrelated areas:
- pupil/student motivation;
- course design;
- curriculum development.

Pupil motivation

From the student's or pupil's point of view, the strength of the module lies in its immediacy. Courses constructed in this way do not stretch interminably before them, to culminate in a distant examination hall some three years or so in the future. Nor do they reach their conclusion at the end of the academic year, or with the coming of the next holidays. Pupils will not require constant reminders about eventual outcomes (good or bad) nor reassurances that if they persist with their studies, complete all the assignments and continue to make steady progress, all will eventually be well. The targets set will be immediate, short-term ones and the feedback that an individual receives will be similarly direct. The precise length of each unit may vary but it will be measured in weeks rather than months.

The nature of these targets is also likely to differ in a modular approach. Rather than the somewhat amorphous and enigmatic aims associated with many traditional courses, those emerging from modular schemes tend to be quite specific and expressed in behavioural rather than abstract terms. In other words, they tell exactly what is expected of them in each unit – what precise skills will be developed and what knowledge they will be called upon to assimilate. Such specificity is, in some cases, a by-product of focusing on a much smaller area of the curricular terrain; in others it is the necessary prerequisite to a free and open selection by the pupils of modules to meet their own individual needs. This may be set out in the form of a 'contract' between teacher and taught.

Criteria-referencing of this kind has led to the emergence of the 'unit credit', awarded to pupils on the successful completion of each module and now being incorporated into leaving certificates in different parts of the country. The *Letter of Credit* and *Letter of Achievement* issued by the Northern Partnership for Records of Achievement (NPRA) is fairly typical (see Curricular Item 1).

This would seem to be a far more realistic approach to continuous assessment than the multifarious files, projects, audio cassettes and sundry course materials recently spawned by so many schemes. Such accreditation will certainly be familiar to anyone who has studied through the Open University (see p 31). Criteria-referencing is also playing a major role in the newer school examinations such as CPVE and GCSE, where 'candidates across the ability range are given opportunities to demonstrate their knowledge, abilities and achievements; that is, to show what they know, understand and can do'.[1]

Active learning

The openness of such modules, with their short-term goals, unambiguous objectives and positive criteria for success, leads to certain assumptions about the kind of relationship that will exist between teacher and taught within them. Conditions such as these both call for, and assist in the development of, a genuinely two-way exchange of ideas. They facilitate an educational dialogue in which the pupil shoulders far greater responsibility for his own learning and the all-important skills of study are developed.

David Hargreaves explains clearly just how this can happen once a course has been modularised:

> Course objectives, instead of existing only in the teacher's mind or the course design, can now be shared with the pupils. If pupils see clearly where they are going, they are more likely to be motivated to make the journey. Once course objectives have been shared beween teacher and pupil, it is easier for teacher and pupils to negotiate the means by which the unit goal can be reached. In other words, there can be joint planning of methods and procedures of work. This takes pupils out of passive roles into active and collaborative roles with the teacher. At the end of the unit, teachers

---

[1]   DES *National Criteria for GCSE* HMSO, 1985, para 16

CURRICULAR ITEM 1
External accreditation of modules (NPRA)

a

LETTER OF CREDIT

R.J. Smithson
Northern High School

has completed successfully the following units of work; a total of

NINE

In support of this letter of credit, as each unit is completed, a statement of achievement is issued to the student by the

LOCAL EDUCATION AUTHORITY

The statement gives details of the requirements for the successful completion of the unit. Where appropriate the statement lists any further achievements which have been validated by the Local Education Authority.

Units Completed

Science at work: pollution
Elementary word processing
Workshop skills: safety and first aid
An introduction to child care
Library skills
Creative writing: short stories
Managing personal income and expenditure
Conservation in an urban area
Control technology: pneumatics

Chairman, Northern Examining Association

b

STATEMENT OF ACHIEVEMENT
Scheme of Unit Accreditation
LEEDS LOCAL EDUCATION AUTHORITY

This unit of work was devised by the Leeds Education Authority and validated by the Northern Examining Association. The title of this unit will appear on a final letter of credit to be issued to the student by the N.E.A

Elementary Word Processing

R.J. Smithson 21st April 1970 of NORTHERN HIGH SCHOOL

In completing this unit the student has:

demonstrated an ability
1. to connect together a microcomputer and its peripherals.
2. to turn on in the correct sequence and handle floppy discs with care.
3. to use a word processor to enter and edit simple text.
4. to use a keyboard accurately as a means of communication.

shown knowledge of
5. the position and function of special keys.
6. the terms, cursor, CPU, VDU, printer, disc drive, floppy disc, data file, backup file, centre and right justification.

had experience of
7. using a Commercial Word Processing package.
8. working in a group and sharing workload.

DIRECTOR OF EDUCATION

DATE 3rd December 1985

a Reproduced by permission of the Northern Partnership for Records of Achievement
b Reproduced by permission of Leeds LEA

and pupils can overtly and jointly evaluate the extent to which unit objectives have been achieved. This helps to motivate pupils for the beginning of the next unit. It also makes it genuinely possible for the pupils to play an active role in curriculum development and evaluation.[2]

The overriding importance of such an approach is further underlined by Her Majesty's Inspectorate who, in *The Curriculum from 5 to 16*, affirm:

> Active learning, and a sense of purpose and success, enhance a pupil's enjoyment, interest, confidence and sense of personal worth; passive learning . . . can lead to frustration and failure . . . The *national primary survey* found that the work children were given to do was better matched to their abilities when teachers employed a combination of didactic and exploratory approaches. The *national secondary survey* pointed to the care needed to avoid teaching styles developing within subjects and across the curriculum as a whole which overemphasise the abstract and the theoretical at the expense of the experimental and the practical: writing at the expense of talking; factual knowledge at the expense of skills and understanding; and narrowly prescribed work at the expense of that in which pupils might use their own initiative.[3]

Teacher motivation

In all these ways the modular approach emphasises student motivation – the creation of an active rather than a passive role for the learner. This may initially involve a considerable investment of time, preparation and energy. The risks may be great. But the rewards, when they come, are enormous and – once an ambience of activity has been created – learning is both easier to sustain and far more conducive for all concerned. The motivation of the teacher, it should not be forgotten, is inextricably bound up with that of the pupils.

An essential distinction

Modules may go a long way to ensure student motivation and a healthy two-way interchange between teacher and taught, but they are not ends in themselves. Were this the case, the programmes to emerge would be fragmentary in the extreme. Modules remain, at best, the building blocks from which a course or a larger area of the curriculum is constructed. It is the manner in which they are brought together, and the relationship that exists between them once this is achieved, that is important.

---

[2]   Hargreaves, D. *Improving Secondary Schools* ILEA, 1984, para 3.11.11
[3]   HMI *The Curriculum from 5 to 16* HMSO, 1985, para 20

Earlier in this chapter (page 4) three examples of modular planning were taken from everyday life: the kitchen, the rocket and the jigsaw puzzle. Closer examination will reveal a sharp division of emphasis between the first one and the other two. This is an essential difference for anyone involved in curriculum planning.

In the case of the kitchen, the modules are completely independent and may be brought together in different configurations; coherence exists in the mind of the constructor. Within the second two modular examples no such variation is possible. The starting point is not an individual choosing the shape and layout he requires, but an overall pattern or design from which all must work. The whole here is nothing more, or less, than the sum of its individual parts.

To reduce all this to the simplest of terms, the analogy of a Lego brick and a jigsaw puzzle piece is useful. The first is a single unit from which no end of products may emerge – a windmill, a fire engine, a tank, a drawbridge, a control tower . . . All of these and many more can be constructed from the same set of bricks. Their uses are limited only by the ingenuity or the imagination of the builder. The jigsaw piece, on the other hand, can occupy one place and one place only within the puzzle. It has a single specific function and this is predetermined. Although a degree of freedom may be permitted in the way it is handled, the user has no control whatsoever over this – indeed, to give too much freedom here would be to destroy the ultimate design; the overall pattern would be incomplete.

Course design

Both of the modular patterns described above have a large part to play in the work of a school or college. Each has much to commend it and the final choice must always rest with the institution wishing to develop its curriculum along these lines. It is, of course, possible to have both approaches operating simultaneously in the same school, either with pupils of different ages or within differing areas of the curriculum. In such circumstances, what is in any case important becomes a vital necessity: that the rationale for each scheme is clearly understood and that its merits have been fully explored.

The second of these approaches (the jigsaw-puzzle approach) views short-term goals as intermediary steps towards the eventual understanding of a subject discipline or some other clearly defined area of the curriculum. Given the correct sequence of modules – which will be determined by the subject-matter being followed – it becomes relatively easy to plot an individual's progress. As the targets are reached, so the pupils grow in confidence, early success leading to progressive mastery of the material and the skills pertaining to it.

There is little that is new about such an approach. It has always had a place in educational theory. Over the last 50 years, however, it has gained added credibility through the work of behaviourists such as Skinner and Watson[4], whose ideas led first to the concept of the teaching machine and then to the classroom use of the microprocessor. This whole process has been sharpened up considerably through modular planning, which encourages the sharing of clear, short-term objectives with the pupils and often involves the introduction of unit credits – referred to earlier – for which external awards are now available.

Such a developmental approach to modules has much to offer the new single system of examining at 16 (GCSE). The influential *Cockcroft Report* on mathematics noted:

> We cannot believe that it can be in any way educationally desirable that a pupil of average ability should for the purpose of obtaining a school leaving certificate be required to attempt an examination paper on which he is able to obtain only about one third of the possible marks. Such a requirement, far from developing confidence, can only lead to feelings of inadequacy and failure.[5]

These ideas are taken up in GCSE through the process of *differentiation* within papers, questions or graded answers. There is a need to distinguish between those parts of the course which are common to all pupils and those which the full potential of the most able among them. One solution might be to stream rigidly from the outset; but this takes little account of late developers or those on the borderline between differentiated groups. Moreover, such a system is open to the criticism of social divisiveness. A more equitable and educationally sound approach would seem to lie in the careful gradation of material in modular form and the progression of the pupils through it in the way described above, until each reaches his individual limits. Such a system also allows for changes in direction once a course has begun, between GCSE and, say, the more vocational CGLI or CPVE variants.

Negotiating the curriculum

The aim of the first approach to modular planning (the 'Lego' pattern) is to place the individual at the very centre of the educational process. It attempts to ensure that his needs are adequately met within the curriculum rather than being constrained by it.

---

[4]   See Child, D. *Psychology and the Teacher* (Holt, Rinehart and Winston, 1977)
[5]   Cockcroft, W. *The Teaching of Mathematics* HMSO, 1984

In such programmes two elements that have been constants in most of the schemes so far considered disappear. Here emphasis is upon choice: pupils are no longer considered as a single group – as they were, for instance, under the scheme advocated by David Hargreaves (see p. 6). Modules also differ. Each one is now completely self-contained and free-standing. A large number are generated and although individuals students may be following the same broad course of study, they can build up the content for themselves. This sometimes leads to radically different combinations. The specialist could be tackling a series of modules which cover one specific area in great depth while, at the same time, the generalist might select those which provide a wide knowledge over the whole field. Those with a practical bent could be conducting action research; the artistic individual might approach the subject through a combination of more creative units.

Great care and attention is required in the planning of such open courses as there is no set order in which the modules will be tackled and the composition of the group will change as each unit comes to an end. It must be possible to link every module with every other one, making no assumptions about what has gone before or what is to follow. This may even apply across a number of separate institutions if the consortia approach is adopted.

The system of accreditation referred to earlier (p. 6) has an important function here, the most signal success of this approach coming with the introduction of TVEI and CPVE. The latter is built around modules of different kinds, the content and sequence of which are almost entirely dependent upon staff-student discussion. The *negotiated curriculum* and the *student profile* are two elements which have emerged from this background into national prominence.

Curriculum development

Quite apart from the contribution that it can make to course planning, the modular approach has much to offer the curriculum as a whole, and its development.

The emphasis placed upon short, concentrated units of work may well suit some subject areas better than the traditional 'drip-feed' approach in which a discipline is taught, in some cases, for just one or two periods each week. In foreign languages, for example, modules lasting up to six weeks may give just the kind of intensive practice that is required at certain points within the course. They might be associated with a visit to France, Germany or Spain, or an exchange scheme. Fieldwork in environmental studies, geography or biology could also be treated in this way, as could work experience or 'industry weeks'.

Units of even shorter duration – lasting no longer than one, two or three periods – are currently being developed by many schools as part of the pastoral curriculum.[6] Such an approach shares with modular planning an emphasis upon activity-work and the negotiation of short-term goals between tutor and pupils. To this may be added the notion of building up a series of such units as and when the pupils are ready for them, and that of 'banking' – in which these modules, once planned and tested, are made available throughout the school, being continually updated and modified in response to their effectiveness. For this to be successful, a fair degree of teamwork and openness is necessary. If this is achieved, there is little reason why the pupils themselves should not be drawn into the process of modular planning and evaluation. (A fairly typical example of one such banked module is given in Curricular Item 15 on page 104).

The short units associated with modular schemes are also ideal test-beds for any curricular innovation a school may wish to introduce. One or more 'dry runs' may be held to ascertain the strengths and weaknesses of the change; a variety of different approaches can be adopted, each one lasting for the time-span of a single module. This will enable a final decision to be made concerning the innovation. Material is far more easily slotted in, or taken out, in response to student need or reaction and the module is far easier to up-date than are sections of a large, unified course.

A further application of this principle is well illustrated by the modular 'taster units' within the TVEI programme shown in Curricular Item 2. Students are here able to make decisions regarding the future development of their courses based not merely upon hearsay or a written statement but on first-hand experience.

Interdisciplinary work

The modular approach also facilitates closer cooperation between subject areas and work of an interdisciplinary nature. Decisions regarding radical modifications of the timetable, such as some of those referred to above, cannot be taken in isolation. The active cooperation of all departments is required. Again, sections of a course presented in one part of the curriculum could well be relevant to students working in other areas. There may even be direct duplication of material. The departmental structure of our schools, however, does not often encourage cross-referencing or syllabuses.

---

[6]   See Baldwin and Wells *Active Tutorial Works* series (Basil Blackwell, 1979–81)

CURRICULAR ITEM 2: Modular 'taster units' (TVEI)

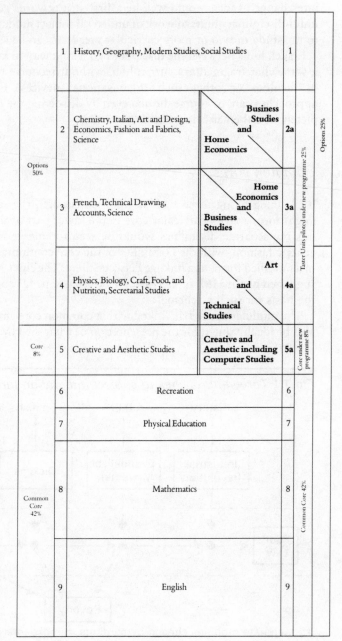

- All students take English, mathematics, physical education and recreation (blocks 6–9).
- All students take creative and aesthetic studies. For students following the new programme, this forms part of a wider programme which also includes computer studies (block 5a).
- Students choosing the new programme follow four taster units (each of twenty weeks duration) in art, technical studies, home economics and business studies during the first year of the programme. In addition, they select two options, one from block 1 and one from either of blocks 2 or 3.
- Taster units in home economics and business studies may be selected from option block 2a or 3a according to which option is chosen in block 2 or 3. For example, students wishing to study chemistry (block 2) should select taster units from block 3a.
- In the second year, students choose a range of modular options providing progression from the taster units; these are built upon in successive years.
- Students not following the new programme select options from blocks 1–4.

Reproduced from *TVEI Review, 1985* (Crown copyright) by permission of the Manpower Services Commission TVEI Unit

Wholesale integration of departments is not envisaged here, but an interchange of ideas could well be a first step towards generating either multi-disciplinary units of work or unilateral subject modules contributing to the study of two or more curricular areas. As can be seen from Figure 1.1. such links between the disciplines go a long way to knitting together a somewhat fragmentary curriculum, without recourse to the formality of faculties or other such organisational devices. Fully integrated approaches can, of course, be achieved by dissolving the disciplines completely in a thematic approach.

Common cores

If planning along these lines is rigorous enough, the modules devised might form a cross-curricular core in the lower part of the school. From this the separate disciplines would be seen to emerge in a natural and generic fashion, with the possibility of the core continuing up the school, in a modified form, as a linkage between them. The eight Areas of Enquiry suggested by the HMI in *Curriculum 11–16* (see p. 41) could well provide the basis for such a scheme.

The modular approach, linked with a common core curriculum, would also be ideally suited for the presentation of what the HMI term 'essential

Fig 1.1 Three approaches to subject integration through modules

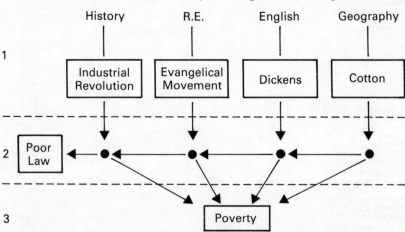

1:   separate modules chosen by students to make *interdisciplinary* programme
2:   different subjects contribute inputs to single *integrated* module
3:   subject boundaries disappear within *thematic* module

issues which are not necessarily contained within subjects, but which need to be included in the curriculum.'[7] These they list as:

Environmental education
Health education
Political education
Economic understanding
The world of work
Careers

What educationists see as 'essential issues' do not always correspond with the views of their pupils, who have ideas of their own. This was recognised by the Coventry Post Primary Working Party, which made the following strong comments and recommendation in its report. *Comprehensive education for life*:

> It is clear that the majority do not wish a continuation of the present schooling process. Many youngsters are bored in the last two years of secondary school: others take the examinations at 16+ without much enthusiasm. Both these groups, which together constitute over 50% of the age group, require a fundamentally different approach. Current work is showing the value for all students of work experience, life skills and personal programmes where positive self-esteem, status and achievement are promoted.
>
> The Working Party concluded that provision up to 18 will need to concentrate on preparing the young for independent living in an increasingly complex adult society. The content of programmes should include life, social and personal skills as well as vocational skills. Direct experience through personal and group activity is needed as well as book learning. These programmes should start at age 14 and allow for sequential and progressive development for each individual which could encompass a mixture of academic, personal, work-related, -full and part-time experiences including with employers. The youngsters should be accorded as nearly as possible adult status: adults with 'L' plates rather than pupils. It is proposed therefore that:
>
> *a system of modular based courses or credits be developed from age 14 which can be extended and built upon to age 18 and including the present examinations in academic subjects.*[8]

Staff development

Breaking down the curriculum into its component parts, either for the purposes of course design or for cross-institutional development, gives greater individual responsibility to the teacher. A module is his to develop

---

[7] HMI *op cit* para 26
[8] Coventry Education Committee *Comprehensive Education for Life* 1982, p. 48

as professionally he feels is for the best, and he will receive far more certain feedback through its specific objectives, unit accreditation, even by students 'voting with their feet', than he will at the end of a broadly-based two-year course which is probably shared with other members of staff. This will help him focus effectively on areas within the unit that have gone badly, while positive feedback may suggest further modules for him or others to develop.

Combined with the kind of interaction which should now be possible with the pupil, modular teaching provides a sound basis both for professional self-analysis and job satisfaction. A modicum of external direction is required for staff development to take place. This is even more marked if the corollary of such an approach is considered – that within these schemes modules may emerge directly from any facet of staff interest, specialisation, skill, or hobby. A curriculum can be envisaged under modular planning that emerges from the individual strengths of those teaching it in direct response to the needs of those who learn through it.

The role of modular planning within managerial training or the induction of newcomers is already being developed in industry (see p. 79). The approach would also seem admirably suited for such purposes within our schools.

Some pitfalls

Modular planning is no panacea. There are pitfalls or dangers associated with each of the major areas in which it has a contribution to make; and it is as well to be aware of these from the outset:

- The pupil/student may be fully motivated, but this counts for little if an adequate system of *monitoring progress* and *recording achievement* had not been devised.
- Courses may be elegantly designed, but little avails if the resulting schemes are so *complex* in their *organisation* that few are able to understand them.
- The curriculum may be developed through modules; it can also become hopelessly atomised or *fragmented* in the process.

For further reading

Two books which graphically illustrate the importance of student motivation are: *In and Out of School* and *Tales Out of School*, both from Youth Education Services. D Hargreaves, in *The Challenge for the Comprehensives* (Routledge and Kegan Paul, 1982), B Baker in *Rescuing the Comprehensive Experience* (Open University Press, 1985) and R J

Campbell in *Developing the Primary School Curriculum* (Holt Saunders, 1985) place this against the wider curricular background.

The response of LEAs to modular approaches can be found in *Improving Secondary Schools* (ILEA, 1984), *Comprehensive Education for Life* (Coventry LEA, 1976), *The Management, Organisational and Curricular Implications of the Implementation of a Modular Approach to the Curriculum and Timetable of Years Four, Five and Six* (A K York for London Borough of Haringey, 1986) and *Stepping Stones, advice on the introduction of a Modular Timetable Structure in the Secondary School* (K Palmer and A Carter, Oxfordshire County Council, 1984). See also 'The Development of Modular Science in Essex and Surrounding Counties' by A R Titcombe (*School Science Review*, June 1983); *What has the Modular Curriculum to Offer?* J Turner (Leicestershire TVEI, 1986) and *Sixteens – Eighteens in Scotland, an Action Plan* (Scottish Education Department, 1983).

Activity learning is thoroughly dealt with in C Rogers' *Freedom to Learn in the Eighties* (Merrill, 1985), in N Evans' *Exploiting Experience* (FEU, 1984) and in L Button's *Developmental Group Work for Adolescents* (Hodder and Stoughton, 1984). R Waterhouse takes these ideas a stage further in *Supported Self Study* (CET, 1983).

The process of change is well handled in *Schools and Curricular Change* by M Holt (McGraw Hill, 1980) and interdisciplinary work by D Warwick in *Integrated Studies in the Secondary School* (Hodder & Stoughton, 1975). Although somewhat costly, S Carroll and P McQuade's *Staff Development Manual* is both practical and comprehensive.

2 The modular transverse

Two somewhat different approaches to modular planning have been identified. The first takes as its starting-point the subject matter to be covered and, like a jigsaw puzzle, breaks this down into manageable units, each of which has a clearly identifiable part to play in the construction of the whole. The other places far more emphasis upon freedom of choice, with individual programmes being constructed from a series of entirely separate and wholly independent units of work in Lego-brick fashion.

Coherence within diversity

These, however, are only two extremities in a wide variation of planning and practice, as Figure 2.1 indicates:

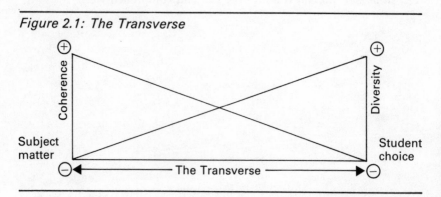

Figure 2.1: The Transverse

Each extremity has particular strengths and weaknesses. The left-hand pole, for instance, is internally *coherent*, stemming as it does from one unified block of material, but could well lack variety of approach and become teacher-dominated. The right-hand supplies the necessary *diversity* but sometimes suffers from a surfeit of choice, leading to curricular fragmentation.

As one moves across the transverse in order to maximise the benefits and minimise the weaknesses, different aspects of the relationship between *teacher, pupils* and *material* will be stressed. These are the component parts of any modular scheme. No value judgement should be made over which is the 'best' and 'worst' approach *per se*. Each will vary and the essence of the difference will depend precisely on the value assigned to *analysis* over *synthesis*, or vice-versa. Modular planning is, above all, a process of achieving the best possible equilibrium of coherence within diversity.

The first decision for any school embarking on a modular scheme, then, relates to the nature of such an equilibrium; at just what point along the transverse does it wish to operate?

Staging posts

At one extremity are those courses in which modules are created by a department, faculty, team or individual in order to make their material more accessible to those being taught. Individual units of work are seen as staging-posts en route through a particular course; vehicles whereby effective learning of a specific kind can take place. They are designed for a special use, be it the teaching of GCSE Physics, A-Level Spanish, a fifth year course on Technical Drawing or a middle-school treatment of Geology. Hence they cannot be taken out of sequence or used in other kinds of configuration.

The pupils are given no choice regarding either the modules they follow or the order in which they will be tackled. The group 'need', as perceived by the teacher, takes precedence, together with a sequence dictated by the nature of the subject-matter to be followed. The group as a whole advances through the syllabus at roughly the same rate along these pre-determined lines.

Such an approach is so fundamental that it has become almost the accepted norm in most of our schools. As such it hardly needs illustration, although the following example from the field of *Study Skills* or *Independent Learning* brings out the salient features quite clearly. Here it is suggested that if a set text has to be read and understood within a certain period, say one term, then the first step is to break it down into manageable sections. It could be decided to tackle it on a weekly basis, in which case the whole is divided into 12 parts and 11 sheets of A4 paper are placed in the appropriate places with the dates by which they must be reached written at the top of each. These will be the sub-targets at which the reader is aiming. When the first section has been completed, the book is put aside and brief notes are written on the paper relating to it. The next section is then begun, which has to be finished by the date on the second piece of paper. When this has been reached the book is once more put away and notes relating to both the first and the second sections written up. And so the student proceeds with gathering confidence through the text.

Early success leading to a progressive mastery of the material or of certain specified skills is a fundamental principle behind this form of planning, with the whole being broken down into sufficiently small units to enable this to happen. Continuity is ensured, as all modules stem from the same basic source and lead naturally one into the other, success leading to further success as the work proceeds.

The staging-posts or sub-targets established in this way are for all pupils and may be related to natural breaks in the school year – half-terms, holidays, etc. Tests might be set at the end of each of these periods, and there could be constant allusions to 'keeping up with' or 'getting behind' schedule, but it is surprising how infrequently teachers share their over-view of the programme with the pupils. Only rarely do they map out the year, or term, ahead, indicating at which points certain sections of the material will come to an end and how each section links with the others that have been planned.

Cueing-in the pupils

Teachers move away from such a dominant position – along the transverse towards a more open approach – when they begin to take classes into their confidence; cueing-in their pupils or sharing with them the basic idea behind their planning. Case Study One describes one way in which the work might be introduced.

CASE STUDY ONE
A Modular Sequence

This year we are looking at the major world religions and how they relate one to another.

We shall begin by examining the characteristics of religion itself and I will outline some of the features they have in common. We will take no more than two weeks over this *first unit*, but it is central to all others.

Then, in week three we move on to the first major component of the course. In it we look especially at Hinduism as the 'parent' religion of the East and how other faiths emerged from it. To do this we shall be using the key features of all religions from Unit

One. This *second unit* will take us five weeks, after which we shall be making some visits to Hindu, Buddhist and Sikh centres in our area. These visits are the *third unit* of our course.

Unit four commences in the New Year and looks at Judaism as the second great 'parent' religion and how Eastern Orthodoxy, Roman Catholicism and Protestantism emerged from it. It will last five weeks, taking us through to half-term and culminating in a practical project based on the parish church. This is *Unit five*.

The whole of the second half of the Spring Term will be devoted to Islam as a 'bridge' between East and West (*Unit six*) and the Summer Term will be spent looking at some of the minor religions of the world – again taking our key features from Unit One. This *seventh unit* completes the course.

Far more than the 'royal we' is used here. The teacher's introduction maps out the design of the course as a whole and indicates why individual modules have been arranged in a certain order, and how they relate one to the other. A skeletal outline such as this actively promotes the learning of pupils who might otherwise have lost their way through a morass of diverse information, and older students will be given an impetus towards what teachers are always asking of them – getting ahead in their study, reading around a subject and relating it to other areas of the curriculum. All this is even more likely to happen if, at the outset, each pupil is given a brief written introduction to the course, together with precise dates for the commencement and conclusion of each module. This should be kept along with the rest of their course material and, to be really effective, it needs to be referred to throughout the year.

Curricular Item 3 is the outline of Yorkshire Television's *Be Your Own Boss* (1982). It presents a model approach, both in the simplicity of its approach and in the clarity with which its sequence of programmes (modules) is set out for viewers.

CURRICULAR ITEM 3:
Setting out the store

Programme One

Introduction (Henry Cooper). This series will help you decide if being your own boss is the right thing for you. At worst maybe we'll help you decide it isn't for you – at best we'll turn you into a high-street champ, and most important, you'll have a job and perhaps you'll create work for others.

A   *The Right Person*

In the first half of this programme various people who run their own businesses are featured. They range from redundant steel workers who are avoiding the dole by running their own foundry, to a lady who has opened a wine bar on the South Bank, creating work for other people.

B   *Customers and Marketing*

In this section businesses are featured which highlight the factors which need to be considered in finding customers and marketing the goods. They range from a Partyplan business where friends can be the customers to an Indian restaurant where the quality of food means that word of mouth guarantees the custom.

Programme Two

A   *Premises*

In this section we examine the pros and cons of working from home. A purpose-built unit for small business people is looked at in detail; an interview with the Manager examines the factors which need to be considered when selecting premises; the flexibility of purpose-built workshops is clearly shown. An example is also given of a businessman who has obvious problems with his premises.

B   *Raising Capital*

Four examples of how money can be raised – from a few hundred pounds to hundreds of thousands of pounds. Some of the problems which these people encountered are covered – including buying equipment, goodwill, and who to approach.

Programme Three

A   *Buying a Business*

This part of the programme looks at what is involved in buying a business and shows some of the many aspects which a potential buyer needs to consider.

B   *Employing Others*

Different aspects of employing people are considered in this section – how to find the right staff, staff who are on an equal footing – everyone's the boss (a Cooperative) and employing people who work away from base.

C   *Bank Manager*

An interview with a Bank Manager illustrates what is expected from a prospective business person. The importance in the way information should be presented is stressed.

Programme Four

A   *Inventions and Ideas*

This programme looks at ideas and inventions. We look at two people who have invented a follow-up to the Rubik Cube, a Welsh hill farmer who has opened up his farm in a novel way and a man with a nappy supply and washing service.

The problems involved with developing an idea are considered; patenting and copyright, making a novel idea work and the importance of costing out the idea.

B   *Receiving Payment*

The problems involved in 'getting on' are looked at including how this affects the continuation of a business. An interview with a Trade Protection Society is included in this programme.

Programme Five

A   *Use of Time and Resources*

In this programme, the personal issues are highlighted: how much time being your own boss involves, the support required from the family, efficient use of resources, etc.

Exporting and the help and advice available from COSIRA and The Small Firms Information Service are also mentioned.

B   *Small Firms Minister*

In the Westminster Studio, the Minister for Small Firms explains what the Government is doing to help small businesses.

Programme Six

A   *Franchising*

Franchising is explained. The potential 'boss' is shown how franchising can provide a unique and ready-made method of becoming your own boss.

B   *Management*

Coping with red tape, VAT returns, insurance and general business management are covered in this part of the programme. It is pointed out that all these things have to be done but that there are ways of doing them efficiently and expediently.

Programme Seven

A   *A Success Story*

This is an example of a firm 'who really got it right'; the programme shows how the firm developed from three men working at home to the building of a £13 million site with expansion abroad. In contrast a firm who might never get off the ground is shown.

B   *Accountant*

An accountant explains how he can help the small businessman.

C   *Conclusion*

The series concludes with advice on how the small businessman can seek help and become the big businessman.

Reproduced with permission from *Open Learning in Action*, Yorkshire Television Enterprises Ltd (see p. 37).

Across the transverse

The teacher now needs to be on guard against pre-specifying the material too tightly or administering it so inflexibly that all spontaneity is lost. It would be ironic if the motivation of the pupils, one of the original aims of such an approach, was lost because – just at the point where their enthusiasm was kindled – they were hurried on to the next module. It would be equally disastrous if, in a sequential scheme, the class – or individuals within it – got completely bogged down at a certain point and, rather than pausing to clear any difficulty, the teacher again hustled them on to the next section.

One reaction here might be to pull back altogether; for a teacher to keep all information regarding the development of a syllabus completely to himself and to ration it out as and when seemed appropriate. A solution more in keeping with the principles of modular planning, however, is to advance a little further along the continuum in the direction that we are already heading. This brings the pupils even closer into the teacher's confidence and actually gives them a degree of control over the speed and development of the course they are following.

Being 'in the know' from the outset regarding the route to be taken through the material, and having had the 'staging posts' along it mapped out beforehand, the class is now in a position to negotiate with the teacher over the treatment of different sections. It may be decided to make detours en route, to take in particularly enjoyable parts of the scenery, or to spend additional time making one's way through the more obstacle-ridden parts of the terrain. But everyone will recognise that this could well mean curtailing other parts of the journey or speeding through later sections of the course. Teacher and class together can then bring themselves back onto the main route at a suitable juncture.

Building-in choice

In the modular planning dealt with so far the pupils have had little say in what they actually learn. They may be shown beforehand where they are going or even brought into the proceedings to negotiate the way forward, but the dual assumption has been that it is the teacher's role to devise the course and that the class as a whole proceeds through it in a uniform fashion.

A first, tentative, move away from this position is represented by those courses where options are available. Many 'A' level syllabuses, for example, permit the study of various alternatives in the second year of the course, and, when 'AS' levels (see p. 64) are introduced,[1] an even greater choice will be available.

In such a course the teacher may consult with the group as a whole over which option they will all follow or, given sufficient flexibility of staffing, allow some to choose one option and some another. It might be possible to devise modules in such a way that – by concentrating on certain key elements within the material – the decision is left until a late point in the course, by which time students may be able to follow more specialised units on their own, or in groups, under the supervision of teachers. The Hargreaves Report recommends the joint teaching of fourth and fifth year classes for this purpose in some schools.[2]

The pivotal point or 'halfway house' in our transverse is reached when the pupils are permitted a clear degree of choice over the material they study or the skills they practice. Put in another way, from this stage onwards the scale begins to tip increasingly in favour of the individual exerting control over his own learning.

---

[1]   DES *AS Levels* HMSO, 1984
[2]   Hargreaves, D. *Improving Secondary Education* (ILEA, 1984) para 3.11.14

But the extremity of the tranverse has not yet been reached. The school will still need to have some say over the choices that are being made, and this is usually achieved through direct modification of one or more of the components listed on p. 19. Thus there may be:

- a change in the *teacher's* traditional *role*, the tutorial function being emphasised.
- some *pre-structuring of the material*, by the use of core modules, for example.
- *guidance of the pupils* through the material by the use of carefully prepared record-cards/sheets;
- or, a *combination* of two or more of these approaches.

Core modules

A method of ensuring that, whatever selection of modules is made, the integrity of the subject or curricular area will be maintained, is through linking them all to a central core. It is usually decided that certain issues are of fundamental importance to the course being followed, or that there are central themes running throughout a particular area of study. Quite obviously, students cannot be permitted to neglect such basic material, which is then incorporated into *key* or *core modules* compulsory to all. The GCSE criteria in Geography, for instance, have five such core areas:

- first-hand study of a small area.
- contrasting themes within the British Isles;
- the UK's relationship with wider groups of nations;
- social and environmental issues;
- the interrelationship between people and environment.

The interaction between a course and the key modules within it is well illustrated by the Southern Region Examination Board's (SREB) Music syllabus for GCSE (see Curricular Item 4).

Two further methods of achieving coherence within fairly divergent modular courses are to be found in the unifying module of the Northern Examining Association's Modular Science course (see Curriculum Item 13) and the overarching project incorporated into Ysgol Emrys ap Iwan's courses (Case Study 7).

The first of these devices is undertaken towards the end of the course and aims to allow students to display a range of skills and abilities developed within it. A single eight- or nine-week module, or two four-week units may be followed, with strong emphasis on skills and experimentation. The project at Ysgol Emrys ap Iwan has the same effect – that of 'drawing together the strands of the modules which belong to a "family" of experiences'.[3]

---

[3]   Pyart, S. *Evaluation of a Modular Curriculum* Ysgol Emrys ap Iwan, 1986, p 6.

CURRICULAR ITEM 4: Core modules in music

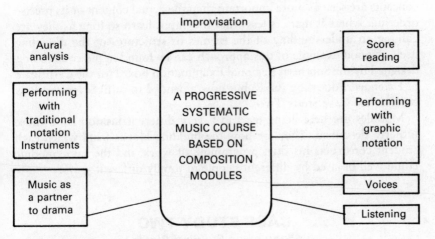

Basic Structure of a Course Module:

A   Aural experience or Musical technique

B   Use of 'A' in composing –

 Assignment to impose order on musical elements (assess).

 Limit resources to stimulate rather than restrict.

C   Perform composition (assess).

D   Listen to reinforce concept and broaden horizons.

E   Aural testing to evaluate (assess) learning.

Reproduced with permission of the Southern Regional Examinations Board from *Supplementary Materials and Notes for GCSE Music* R. Evernden, 1985.

Cafeteria curriculum

Great advances have been made along the transverse towards a child-centred approach but, as already noted, the material is still essentially in the teacher's hands. Choice is limited and the conditions in which it is made are carefully circumscribed. Only when the emphasis shifts away from this situation to one in which each individual is given direct control over the construction of a programme of work can radical changes begin to occur. This is usually accompanied, in the centre sections of the transverse at least, by careful tutorial guidance – either from members of the department concerned or, in schools with well-developed pastoral systems, by a personal tutor. Negotiation of this kind is often associated with the compilation of an on-going profile, or 'goal setting based on mutual agreement'.[4]

---

[4]   White, R., Pring, R. and Brockington, D. *The 14–18 Curriculum: Integrating CPVE, YTS, TVEI?* Youth Services Ltd, 1985, p 22.

More open approaches are possible in areas of the curriculum where concepts are seen as more important than the actual content or its precise ordering; where it matters less what the pupils learn so long as they are gaining an understanding of the themes or structures of the discipline itself. A good example of this approach can be found in the courses first designed by the Southern Regional Examination Board for the Certificate of Extended Education (CEE) but now amended to fulfil Seventeen Plus criteria (see Case Study Two).

Modules are here being used in a very different fashion from those hitherto described. They are now the building blocks from which each student constructs his own programme of work and the same module could well be used by different people in totally different ways.

CASE STUDY TWO
Modules as Building Blocks

There are six large Areas of Study: *Science and Technology; Mathematics and Computer Studies; Design Centred Studies; Humanities; Communication;* and *European Studies.* To comply with examination regulations, students are required to choose any three modules from within, or even across, these six areas and to follow them either sequentially or concurrently.

The unit from *Communication* entitled *The artist and his work,* for example, could be put together with those on *The study of a particular theme* and *The performance of a play* to give one slant or fulfil one need. Added to those on *Television genre* and *The mass media,* a rather different pattern is produced. Taken outside this particular Area of Study and followed alongside modules on *Eastern Europe* and *Modern European Literature* gives a further slant, whilst utilising a module on *Architectural studies* from the *Humanities* Area could provide still futher dimensions to any combination of those already mentioned.

As each Area of Study consists of some thirty or so modules, the range of possibilities is enormous!

Learning is becoming infinitely more active; the pupils are making information their own rather than receiving it at the pace dictated by the teacher in a carefully guarded sequence of his choice.

Four 'pathways' traced through a modular course within the Welsh school referred to on p. 26 indicate precisely what is possible (see Curricular Item 5).

The traditional *table d'hôte* type of offering begins to give way to something approaching an *à la carte* menu. The age-old dilemma over

CURRICULAR ITEM 5
Modular pathways, Ysgol Emrys ap Iwan, Aberele

JAMES

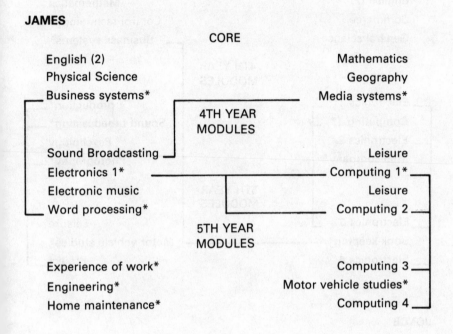

CORE

English (2)	Mathematics
Physical Science	Geography
Business systems*	Media systems*

4TH YEAR
MODULES

Sound Broadcasting — Leisure
Electronics 1* — Computing 1*
Electronic music — Leisure
Word processing* — Computing 2

5TH YEAR
MODULES

Experience of work* — Computing 3
Engineering* — Motor vehicle studies*
Home maintenance* — Computing 4

JANE

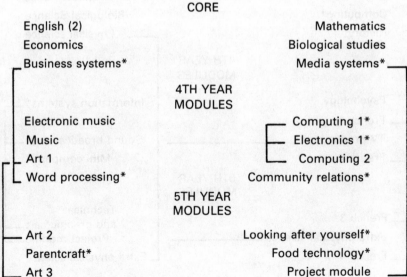

CORE

English (2)	Mathematics
Economics	Biological studies
Business systems*	Media systems*

4TH YEAR
MODULES

Electronic music — Computing 1*
Music — Electronics 1*
Art 1 — Computing 2
Word processing* — Community relations*

5TH YEAR
MODULES

Art 2 — Looking after yourself*
Parentcraft* — Food technology*
Art 3 — Project module

JOHN

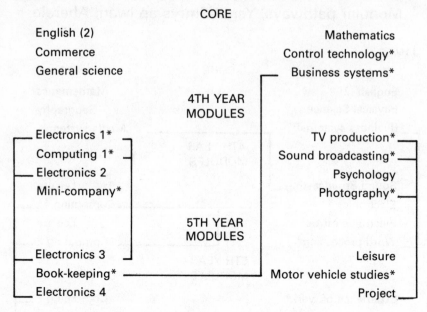

CORE

English (2)	Mathematics
Commerce	Control technology*
General science	Business systems*

4TH YEAR
MODULES

Electronics 1*   TV production*
Computing 1*   Sound broadcasting*
Electronics 2   Psychology
Mini-company*   Photography*

5TH YEAR
MODULES

Electronics 3   Leisure
Book-keeping*   Motor vehicle studies*
Electronics 4   Project

JOYCE

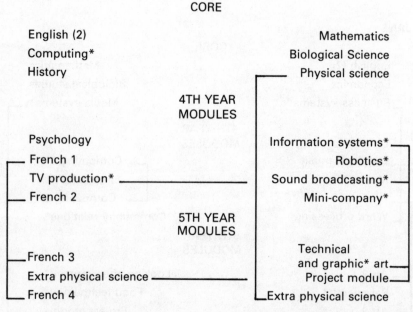

CORE

English (2)	Mathematics
Computing*	Biological Science
History	Physical science

4TH YEAR
MODULES

Psychology   Information systems*
French 1   Robotics*
TV production*   Sound broadcasting*
French 2   Mini-company*

5TH YEAR
MODULES

French 3   Technical
                          and graphic* art
Extra physical science   Project module
French 4   Extra physical science

Reproduced with permission from S Pyart, *Evaluation of a Modular Curriculum* Ysgol Emrys ap Iwan, 1986, pp 19–25 devising a programme that responds to individual need approaches a solution in what could be termed the 'cafeteria curriculum'.

Negotiating the curriculum

Having travelled this far across the modular continuum away from approaches in which both teacher and curricular material were in the ascendancy, it is now but a short step to the opposite pole.

This is reached when teacher and student consult together in a completely open fashion over the kind of work which would be most suitable. A curriculum is then jointly negotiated, tailored entirely to suit the individual's requirements. In colleges of further education such an approach is built into the organisational framework. Work here is based on *courses* constructed of units of work which are derived from the various departments, faculties, schools, etc. Part-time staff may be appointed to meet a short-term need. A *matrix* system of management is often used to facilitate such an approach, there being a division between those responsible for interviewing and assessing student need and those responsible for devising the units of work. In actuality the same member of staff frequently operates in a dual capacity, much in the way that in schools a teacher may at the same time be Head of History and a fourth-year tutor.

The most well-known use of this approach is, of course, the *Certificate of Pre-Vocational Education* (CPVE). Students here develop ten core skills through a series of modules – *Introductory, Exploratory* and *Preparatory* – which become progressively more vocational in emphasis and practical in orientation. These cover five occupational 'families' and an individual programme, negotiated between the student and his tutor, may concentrate on just one of these or cover a combination of two or more. The 'Preparatory stage' does not necessarily have to be reached in order to gain a certificate and this, through a skilful use of modular planning, gives CPVE its broad, comprehensive approach (see Curricular Item 6).

Distance learning

Modular approaches as open and flexible as this are ideally suited to those courses, like CPVE, which attract students from widely differing backgrounds, possibly looking for very different outcomes as a result of their studies. Distance learning is a case in point. Here, to take an Open University example, the units which comprise E323, *Management and the school*, could be followed by teachers, governors, lecturers, LEA advisers or interested parents. Of these, some may be taking the course as part of an on-going programme leading to a degree, or perhaps to build up credits towards an advanced diploma. Others could be taking

CURRICULAR ITEM 6
Flexible modules, CPVE

HOW MODULES RELATE TO CATEGORIES AND CLUSTERS

CATEGORY	CLUSTER	
AN INTRODUCTORY MODULE	DOUBLE EXPLORATORY MODULES	PREPARATORY MODULES
Business and Administrative Services	Control of Organisations Services to Business	Audio Typewriting Typewriting Word Processing Book-keeping Accounting Procedures Clerical Services Enterprise Skills Reception Duties
Technical Services	Information Technology and Micro-Electronic Systems Service Engineering	Product Design Engineering Drawing Electronics Electrical and Electronic Systems Micro-Electronic Systems Information Processing Data Handling Computing Motor Vehicle Engineering Engineering Processes Installation and Maintainence
Production	Manufacturing Craft-based Activities	Physical Science Materials Technology Fittings and Furnishings Design and Graphics Fabrication and Welding Building Construction Construction Service Installations Finishes and Decoration
Distribution	Retail and Wholesale	Customer Service Merchandising Wholesaling and Warehousing Stock Control Buying Display
Services to People	Health and Community Care Recreation Services Hospitality including Food and Accommodation	Childcare Nutrition Human Development Health Care Services Health Studies Care of the Handicapped Care of Elderly First Aid Geography of Tourism Travel and Tourism Leisure Services Beauty Therapy Food Preparation and Production Home Economics Food Service Accommodation Services Home Management and Institutional Management

**Some Preparatory modules may be of value to students in more than one category.
This diagram will change as modules for new clusters are added.**

Reproduced with permission from CPVE 5, March 1985

it purely to increase professional skills, or from interest alone. The way in which individual modules may be combined with others to form coherent courses of study is further illustrated in Curricular Item 7.

Agencies involved in distance learning and teaching usually stress that attendance at tutorials is important, but not compulsory. This means that the course designers cannot rely upon such participation as part of their programmes. The modules they produce have therefore to be quite explicit about the nature of each unit, how it fits in with others in the series, and the range of skills it sets out to develop. Fragmentation of content and narrowness of vision must be avoided, but this can only be done vicariously – at second-hand.

Flexilearning

The most flexible of such courses are those which shed all the traditional barriers to learning and – with them – most of the conventional contexts. Figure 2.2 shows how Roger Lewis summarises these[5].

Although elements of the modular approach can prove helpful, such schemes extend beyond the limits of even the broad transverse along which we have been travelling (see Case Study Three).

Figure 2.2

Barrier	Example
Physical	location of course
Time	time of classes times of exams
Educational	content of course sequencing of content method of delivery inappropriate objectives
Individual	lack of awareness of what is available lack of confidence entry requirements
Financial	cost of travel and fees cost of release from employment cost of course materials[5]

---

5   Lewis, R. 'What is Open Learning?' in *Open Learning* Vol 1, No 2 (June 1986) p 6.

CURRICULAR ITEM 7
Modular choice within The Open University

Course code and title	Page	Brief description	This course is particularly relevant to	Previous knowledge of subject area required	Form of assessment	Certification	Support services	Duration of course & approx. hours of study	Price
PSYCHOLOGY									
DS262 Introduction to psychology	105	Introduces the different approaches and methods in psychology and helps develop the basic skills involved in psychological research		□	written work + exam	Certificate of Satisfactory Completion	tutor + counsellor + summer school	Feb-Oct 240 hrs	£195
D307* Social psychology: development, experience and behaviour in a social world	105	The primary purpose of this course is to provide insight into social behaviour		□	written work + projects + exam	Certificate of Satisfactory Completion	tutor + counsellor + computing facilities	Feb-Oct 420 hrs	£285
D309 Cognitive psychology	105	An advanced course which introduces students to the current theories and methodologies used to study higher mental processes		□□□	written work + exam	Certificate of Satisfactory Completion	tutor + counsellor + summer school + computing facilities	May be available from 1987	
PD561 Open guides to psychology: Basic cognitive processes	106	Preparation notes for passing psychology examinations in basic cognitive processes: perception, attention, learning and memory	students of psychology courses	□				any time	£5.95

* Course description for D307 is given on facing page (p. 35)

CURRICULAR ITEM 7 (cont)

Social psychology: development, experience and behaviour in a social world
Course Code D307

Fee: £285 Full credit Third level
Audio-cassette Video-cassette Transferable towards a BA degree

This course is designed for both specialist psychologists and for those whose interests are in social science, education, arts and humanities. It is, however, a third level course and will be considerably more accessible to those who have studied some psychology or sociology before.

The aims of the course are to promote an understanding of social behaviour, and personal experience in the contemporary social world. A range of theories will be discussed in their historical and political contexts and related to assumptions about the nature of man and society. The course will teach research methods and use practical project work to give the student an opportunity to develop research skills and a critical awareness of methodological problems.

The early part of the course is structured around the chronological development of individuals. It questions the function of families from a variety of perspectives and applies systems theory to the processes which occur in normal and pathological family interactions. It also discusses the nature/nurture debate and theories of child socialization. The social and communicative skills that are necessary for a child to become a member of the social world, including acquisition of language and its use in establishing social identity, are explored. The progress of personal relationships, the nature of consciousness and the way our experience changes through the life cycle relate course material to the personal experience of students. There is then a shift away from an individualistic perspective. Attempts to generalize about people's world views and their attitudes are used to introduce a longitudinal study of political socialization of young adults and their decision on how to vote in a General Election. The experience and effects of group membership, intergroup relations and crowd behaviour are examined and lead into a discussion of social movements and change.

Reproduced with permission from *Continuing Education Guide* Open University, 1985, pp 25, 105.

CASE STUDY THREE
Open Learning

KOLAP, the *Kingston Open Learning Action Programme* . . . is an Open Tech scheme for training industrial supervisors. Open learning programmes are set up and run by college-based tutors for supervisors nominated by their companies. The scheme is relatively open on:

What?	The learner negotiates learning objectives with his tutor and line manager.
How?	Routes can be negotiated on an individual or group basis.
When?	Start, finish and pace are all negotiable.
How is the learner doing?	Progress is reviewed periodically through discussion with tutor, line managers and other learners.
Who can help the learner?	A number of different supporters are built into the scheme, including tutors, line managers and other learners.

Midtech, an Open Tech delivery system covering three counties in East Anglia. Midtech works through a network of resource centres based in educational or industrial organisations . . . Midtech is relatively open on:

Who?	Anyone may approach Midtech for a course.
How?	Midtech can deliver via many routes, using different methods and media.
When?	Individuals can start and finish at any time.[6]

Reproduced with permission from Lewis, R *What is Open Learning?* CET, 1984 p 6.

For further reading

Matters covered in this chapter can be more fully explored in Schools Council Working Paper 70, *The Practical Curriculum* (1981) and W A Reid and D F Walker's *Case Studies in Curriculum Change* (Routledge and Kegan Paul, 1975). At classroom and tutorial level *What Shall we Teach?* by M Shipman (Hodder & Stoughton, 1985) and the *Active Tutorial Work* series, edited by Wells, Baldwin and Smith (Basil Blackwell, 1979-81 are all useful.

An outline of how more open approaches were developed in one school is given in J Watts' *The Countesthorpe Experience* (Allen and Unwin,

---

[6]   Ibid, pp 8–9. See also Harris, D. *Openness and Closure in Distance Education* (Falmer Press, 1987).

1977) and T Burgess edits an interesting collection of papers on this general theme – *Education for Capability* (NFER/Nelson, 1985).

Details of CPVE are to be found in the various course manuals (1984-) and R Lewis has edited an invaluable set of case-studies, *Open Learning in Action* (CET, 1984). The journal *Open Learning* is available from Longman three times a year (February, June and November).

Series 1 and 2 of *Be Your Own Boss* (see pages 21–24) are available on video cassette at £55 each, from Geoff Foster, Yorkshire Television, Television Centre, Leeds LS3 1JS.

3 Modules and the core curriculum

Modular planning is sufficiently flexible to be used in schools or colleges of every kind and with students of all ages. It does not specify a universal format for modules, prescribe how they should be brought together or dictate the teaching methods to be adopted. Full use should be made of this adaptability; the modular approach decided upon can be made to fit precisely the overall aims of the institution into which it is being introduced.

Infant modules

Informality and a spontaneous reaction to individual need are the hallmarks of infant education. Modular approaches are not often to be found here but, if they are, usually emerge from the right-hand extremity of the transverse on page 18. Generalisations are always dangerous, yet it seems that both the youngest and the most mature – that is, the rising fives and adults on correspondence or Open Tech courses – share the benefits of schemes that are remarkably similar in design and approach.

Examples are not easy to come by, but Case Study Four, from a school in the north-west, gives a very good idea of just what is possible at this stage.

CASE STUDY FOUR
Modules in the Infant School

The school was faced with twin problems – an increasing population and severe limitation of space. A balanced programme of rich, tactile experiences was vital for the five-year-olds, yet a full provision of sand, water, play, toy areas, etc, was not possible.

The first step towards a solution was to decide just what experiences of this kind were really necessary and then to designate specific parts of the building for such purposes. There followed some discussion of the programming of the work, leading to a 'cycling round' of the pupils in order to give a fair balance of experience to each. This at once robbed the exercise of much of its spontaneity. Instead of coming to a certain activity as and when they felt the need, the children were marshalled round all the areas in strict rotation, having to begin 'play' or work with sand, water and so on at a precise time and finish possibly just as they were getting interested. There was little relationship between this programming and the attention-span, moods or day-to-day interests of individuals. Motivation lapsed and the school became a less happy place.

It was then decided to try an experiment. Supposing each child was to choose which activity he wanted to do, how long he would do it, and in what order the various experiences were to be followed? Teachers would be there to supervise the different areas, together with parental help, and there would, of course, be plenty of time spent together at 'base'. But how could the numbers wishing to participate in each activity be regulated? How would an equitable balance of such modules be achieved? Above all, how could some record of the work done be kept?

The answer was to colour-code each area. Red was for water, blue for sand and so on. Just sufficient sashes of each colour for the various activities were made up and hung on pegs in a central position. The children could take a coloured sash, go to the specified area, work there for as long as they felt the need and then return the sash to its correct hook. They could tell at a glance by the number and colour of the remaining sashes which places were vacant and select another activity. The staff could keep a watchful eye on individuals who spent too long in certain areas or were changing activities too frequently.

Meanwhile, a system of coloured counters could be used to give a visual indiciation each week as to just how long each child had spent on the various activities. From this evidence the teachers could build on what had been done and steer individuals into comprehensive series of experiences.

The scheme was a great success. Not only did it combine freedom of choice with coherence of programming, but there was a clear, simple and direct method of monitoring results. As well as building up a range of first-hand experiences upon which later academic progress would depend, the children were also gaining valuable insights into other, less tangible aspects of education – sharing, co-operation, decision-making and choice.

Primary approaches

The primary school takes its basic characteristics from its size – few have more than 500 children – and the devolution of responsibility for the

education of each group almost entirely into the hands of a single classroom teacher. The theme teaching, or an approach through topics, and the
'integrated day' have become synonymous with schooling of this kind,
the English 'open approach' attaining international renown in the years
following the *Plowden Report.*[1]

Modular planning most frequently adopts this format when practised
within such a context. A variety of skills, approaches, subject matter and
resources are brought to bear on a topic of general but immediate interest.
The whole class is likely to be involved, but the emphasis is usually on
experiential learning through individual discovery or group work. The
children's attention is thus concentrated for a relatively short period of
time and there is some sharing of general aims. Any rigorous pre-planning
through specific objectives, though, is felt by many to be inappropriate
at such a level or unsuitable for 'discovery' methods of this kind.

In recent years there has been some concern that 'essential areas of
understanding and experience' could be neglected through over-emphasis
on schemes such as these. These essential areas were listed by HMI in
1978 as:

- Language and literacy
- Mathematics
- Science
- Aesthetics (including PE)
- Social abilities (including RE)[2]

The *Bennett* research of 1976[3] questioned the benefits conferred through
Plowden methodology, while the Leicestershire *ORACLE* investigation
seemed to indicate that in some schools things were continuing much as
they previously had done, beneath the guise of informal methods.[4] More
recently still, in *Teaching Quality*, the DES have reminded those responsible for teacher training about the importance of subject specialism at
primary level.[5]

The difficulties of adopting such a system within the primary school
– the small size of the institution, lack of resources, unavailability of
specialists in certain key areas and the employment of them as generalist
classroom teachers once they have been appointed – together with the
necessity of ensuring that a 'common core' of activities is maintained, all
point to modular solutions.

Here the specialist could work either with individual members of staff
or with groups of teachers on short, quite explicit units of work, each

[1]   *Children and their Primary Schools* (The Plowden Report), HMSO, 1967
[2]   HMI *Primary Education in England* HMSO, 1978
[3]   Bennett, N. *Teaching Styles and Pupil Progress* Open Books, 1976
[4]   Galton, M. and Simon, B. *Progress and Performance in the Primary School* Routledge
      and Kegan Paul, 1980
[5]   DES *Teaching Quality* HMSO, 1983

of which would cover one, two or three days , or occupy – say – half a day a week over a half-term period. These units could be presented to individual classes or groups of classes, with the teachers involved working either as a teaching team or covering the work done by one another. Specialised resources, such as laboratory equipment, projectors or a pottery wheel could be equitably shared and the spirit of Plowden applied through joint preparation of workcards or sheets from which group-centred activities could be developed. The essence of such material would be a systematic approach to the concepts within each area of work and the sharing of experience between all concerned (see pp. 215/6).

Core curricula

In the lower part of the secondary school emphasis is usually upon the building up of a broad general education, once again giving access to 'essential areas of understanding and experience', here carefully structured through the departmental or faculty system.

The 1980 White Paper *A Framework for the School Curriculum* presented this in purely subject terms:

- not less than 10% of the time was to be spent on English and Mathematics;
- between 10% and 20% on Science;
- not more than 20% on Modern Languages;
- Religious Education and PE to complete the 'core'[6]

The 'Red Book' published three years earlier, though, was somewhat more liberal. Eight general 'Areas of experience' were suggested:

- the Aesthetic/Creative
- the Ethical
- the Linguistic
- the Mathematical
- the Physical
- the Scientific
- the Social/Political
- the Spiritual

This, the HMI wrote, was:

A checklist . . . for curricular analysis and construction . . . It does not in itself demand any one way of teaching or model of timetabling or pattern of internal school organisation . . . It could be realised through a familiar-looking programme of single subjects, or through forms of interdisciplinary work, or with a combination of both; or it could lead to novel groupings and titles of studies.[7]

---

6   DES *A Framework for the School Curriculum*, HMSO, 1980
7   HMI *Curriculum 11–16* HMSO, 1977, p6

More recently still, a series of readable pamphlets from the same source have presented the basic structure of each major subject area and indicated how this fits into *The Curriculum 5 to 16* as a whole[8], whilst *Better Schools*[9] gives the DES' most recent thinking on the content of the curriculum. Of the above list, *Aesthetics, Mathematics,* the *Physical* and the *Scientific* remain more or less intact. The Spiritual and the Ethical, however, are gathered once more within the *Religious Education* fold, the Social and the Political are combined to form *Humanities, Foreign Languages* come in (for most students) instead of Linguistics, whilst *English* (including *Literature*) is mentioned by name and *Practical Studies* completes the tally.

Such a structuring of experience does seem to be of major importance at this stage, no matter how it is achieved, as does access to all the subject disciplines from which a selection will later be made. It is unwise to undermine the process through too early or too liberal a choice of options, yet if choice is to feature at all within the curriculum, early practice of decision-making is surely essential.

At this level, however, choice could take place *within* rather than *between* subject areas. Group work is not uncommon, and the rudiments of a modular approach could well be introduced within such a framework, incorporating as it does a sharing between teacher and taught of the nature of the discipline, the precise contract to be followed, the ordering of such material, and explanation as to how and why it has been broken down in this way. All this could be combined with carefully controlled choice between units of work. Courses constructed in such a way would be complete in themselves, ensuring that all following them benefitted from the experience of a totally rounded and balanced curriculum regardless of the options taken up in the Fourth Year.

Departmental approaches

Modular schemes such as those outlined above will differ considerably, according to the nature of the subject being studied. Indeed, one of the great merits that this approach shares with other curricular innovations is that it throws the planners back to first principles; it requires them to reconsider the precise nature of their discipline, the contribution that it makes to the work of the school, and how this relates to what else is going on in other subjects. This is all the more important at a time when a major complaint is that:

> Although we speak of a common core curriculum operating in many schools already and shared by them (leading some to claim that there is already a

---

8   HMI *Curriculum Matters* (5–16) series HMSO, 1985
9   DES *Better Schools* HMSO, 1985, para 66

national common curriculum of sorts) we find upon more detailed scrutiny that History or Science or Mathematics mean very different things in different schools, even in schools within a mile or so of each other.[8]

The central question facing any department contemplating a modular approach, then, relates to the very essence of its work. Is it, for example, *linear* by nature, with the later stages being wholly dependent upon what has gone before? Is it even more *stratified* than this, with Stage One leading directly into Stage Two, and Stage Three emerging from a combination of both the earlier ones? Most subjects within the curriculum used to be treated in this manner, but now many place more emphasis upon the central themes running throughout or the key concepts that give the discipline its characteristic shape and style.

If this is the case the approach is more *cumulative* in its effect. Here it matters little in which order the content is followed, provided that it is dealt with thoroughly and obeys a certain inner consistency, and that each set of results is completely understood by those following the course. The *Place, Time and Society Project*[10] for instance, comes out with a list of four interlocking sets of objectives – intellectual; social; physical; and personal, together with two types of key concepts. *Methodological* concepts concentrate on similarity/difference, continuity/change, causes/consequences; *substantive* concepts focus on communication, power, values/beliefs and conflict/consensus.

What if the work of a department is of a *practical* nature, with an overt emphasis upon the development of specific skills, or is predominantly creative or *experiential* in its approach? Or if it consists of an admixture of all these approaches? Depending upon the answers given to questions such as these, modules will be utilised in different ways and programmes sequenced accordingly. As will be seen in Chapter Five, the closer the relationship between individual modules within a scheme, the more overall planning will be required; the more independent its individual units, the looser this can be.

Within the faculty

The common core is facilitated in many schools by the establishment of a faculty system. This seeks to give expression to the basic areas of human experience by formally bringing together hitherto separate subject divisions into larger clusters with generic titles such as 'Communication studies', 'Expressive arts', 'Humanities', 'Science and mathematics', etc.

---

[10] Blyth *et al Curriculum Planning in History, Geography and Social Sciences*, Bristol, 1976, p18

Figure 3.1 indicates how different arrangements of disciplines to make up a faculty can present differing curriculum patterns which, in turn, call for alternative approaches to modular planning.

One of the departmental heads from within the faculty is usually designated its leader – sometimes a rota is drawn up for this purpose – courses now being jointly planned and run in a fully independent manner.

An example of what can be achieved in terms of curricular development through an astute use of faculties can be seen in Case Study Five, from Hemsworth High School, West Yorkshire.

Figure 3.1

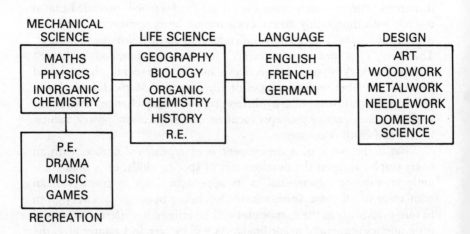

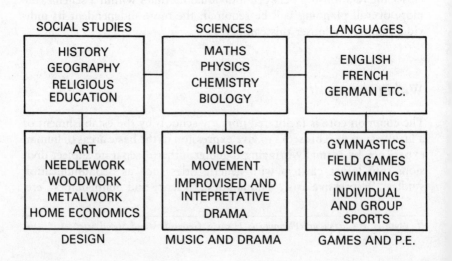

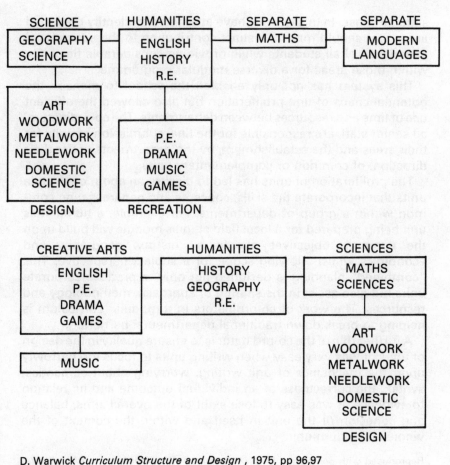

D. Warwick *Curriculum Structure and Design* , 1975, pp 96,97

CASE STUDY FIVE
The use of co-ordinators at Hemsworth High School,
West Yorkshire

The large-scale development of modular courses, both subject and interdisciplinary based, has required a revision of existing curricular structures at Hemsworth to ensure cohesion and balance within the curriculum. In order to guarantee each student a balanced education, co-ordinators have been appointed in Humanities and Expressive Arts. One of their many functions has been to join the co-ordinator of science in a team approach to planning and implementing unit accreditation, that makes both conceptual and organisational sense. In this way we have attempted to identify the broad areas that should make a distinct contribution to the educational experience of all students while providing considerable flexibility within those areas for a diverse modular programme.

This system has not only enabled the school to manage the potential chaos of unit proliferation but also allowed the efficient use of time and resources between departments. The co-ordinators, all senior staff, are responsible for the final submission of units for their areas and the establishment, by the departments under their direction, of common or complementary units.

The proliferation of units has led to discussion about open style units that incorporate the skills, concepts and generalisation common within a group of departments. For example, a humanities unit being prepared for a local field studies module will build upon the common objectives shared by history, geography and economics whilst allowing scope for a subject perspective. This "combined" planning is designed not only to produce corporate units but also assist in the sharing of approach, methodology and resources. The work of co-ordinators in a modular curriculum is helping to break down traditional departmental barriers.

A further role of the co-ordinator is to ensure quality in the design of units. It was very easy when writing units to focus too narrowly upon the mechanics of unit writing, worrying about semantics, syntax, the correctness of an individual outcome and its relation to evidence. It was easy to lose sight of the overall aims, balance and cohesion of the unit in itself and within the context of the whole curriculum unit.

Reproduced with permission from *Unit Accreditation, Problems and Possibilities* (Hemsworth School, 1986)

One danger that must be avoided in the creation of faculties is the concentration of too much unilateral power into their hands. If this is the case, unlike those at Hemsworth, they could become separate entities in their own right, insular and inward-looking. Within each one of them there might then be mutual understanding and an integration of ideas, but at the expense of inter-faculty co-operation and curricular unity.

Across the curriculum

Departments or faculties might form a valuable system through which experience is channelled, but the core curriculum must not be allowed to degenerate into a series of separate blocks all operating in isolation. Presumably, the decision to divide the curriculum in this way was taken on rational grounds and the part to be played by each section carefully considered. Such an interrelationship really needs to be shared with the pupils if they are to get anything out of it.

This could be done within the tutorial system, or by inviting the relevant faculties or departments to create short modules which extend their disciplines in broad terms across the curriculum, rather along the lines suggested by the eight epistemological areas outlined in *Curriculum 11– 16*. Incorporated here would probably be 'those aspects of education which are not simply identified with particular specialist subjects' and 'new' subjects often requiring a different perspective across the curriculum.'[11]

HMI list these as being:

Environmental education, which can help pupils to develop an awareness, appreciation and understanding of their surroundings . . .

Health education, essential for pupils' physical and moral well-being . . .

Information technology, which is having a profound effect on pupils whose adult lives will be in the 21st century . . .

Political education, important if pupils are to understand the forces, issues and processes at work in society . . .

Education in *Economic understanding* . . . helping pupils to come to understand the economic system and general factors which influence it, some of them contentious . . .

Preparing young people for the *World of work* . . . skills and attitudes which enhance their opportunities and provide a sound basis of competence and commitment for their future lives and work . . .

Careers education . . . a need to broaden their horizons so that they do not unthinkingly fall into traditional attitudes.[12]

The modular approach, with its short-term units planned for clearly defined purposes, is probably the only way in which such areas can be introduced satisfactorily at this level.

Study skills

An area not mentioned above, but deserving special attention in modular planning is the process of learning how to learn – the skills of study itself.

---

[11]   HMI *Aspects of Secondary Education in England and Wales*, HMSO, 1979, para 200, 201

[12]   HMI *The Curriculum from 5 to 16* HMSO, 1985, para 13–15

Three assumptions lie behind the lack of attention given to this important aspect of education until comparatively recently.

The first is the belief that such a basic grounding either has, or ought to have, been given by those teaching within the stratum directly below. Such a belief is expressed from top to bottom within the system – from the university lecturer, amazed that his students are unable to organise their own studies without the pressure of some extrinsic sanction, through to the infant school teacher, who wonders what the parents have been up to in not ensuring that the basics have been established. Even where the elements of self-directed study have been inculcated at a lower level, there seems litle reason for not developing them still further. They are not static, and may even atrophy through lack of use. Such skills are vital for any modular scheme both intrinsically, at the level we are now considering, and as a preparation for more sophisticated forms of planning that may be introduced higher up the school.

The second reason for past neglect of this important aspect of schooling seems to have been incomprehension on the part of teachers that pupils actually require anything quite so basic. Surely note-taking, finding information from a book, using a library or preparing a homework schedule are matters of common sense? At times, teachers seem to have adopted an attitude of 'We muddled through, so why can't you?'

Such 'common sense' matters, however, do not come naturally to the children. In the past pupils have all too often been left to acquire these skills in a wholly haphazard fashion – if at all. Added to those cited above might be: the use of a dictionary; note making; report writing; the Dewey system; the conditions of study; revision, etc. If we genuinely believe in the structuring of knowledge, be this through modules or otherwise, skills such as these need to be at the pupils' disposal – not withheld from them, for whatever reason.

Third, there is a belief that skills such as these are best taught within subject areas, where they can be readily related to the content being followed. Those who subscribe to this belief maintain that attention will thus be focused on them from a variety of different sources, and the pupils will come to see their importance. There is great strength in this argument, but it is a theoretical one. The plain fact, as attested by those teaching at sixth-form level and beyond, is that such a process does not take place or, if it does, remains remarkably ineffective in its outcome. Students do not seem to have grasped these small-scale yet vital skills and are not using them in their studies. As with so many of the really important aspects of education, it is assumed that they are being catered for in all sections of the school, whereas it could be that they are practised in none. This argument alone should ensure that, in future, modules of this kind are introduced as part of the core curriculum for all pupils and that they are developed through practice throughout the period of secondary education.

Three types of study skills can be identified:
- *General skills*, such as those mentioned above (note-taking, library skills, etc)
- *Subject-specific skills*, which will, of course be dealt with within the relevant departments (conducting experiments, analysing a poem, etc)
- *General skills* that can be *related to* the work of *departments* in different ways (essay writing, fieldwork, etc). It should not be forgotten that comparison and contrast are excellent teaching methods, so this does not necessarily mean that such skills should be tackled separately.

Of course, general agreement needs to be reached as to which skills fit into which categories and plans made accordingly.

The pastoral curriculum

Reference has already been made (p. 27) to the role of the tutor as possibly being the person best placed to make links between the work being done by each pupil across the curriculum. In completely open schemes, where individual selection from a large number of modules is invited, the tutorial function becomes of paramount importance. Here a comprehensive knowledge of the units available needs to be coupled with counselling skills of a high order and it is difficult to envisage the development of such free-standing, independent modules without the requisite tutorial support.

Such matters will be dealt with more fully in Chapters 9 and 10, but here it should be noted that modular planning has a significant contribution to make to the pastoral curriculum itself. The short, dynamic units which together constitute 'active tutorial work' (see p. 12) need to be planned by the pastoral staff as a whole under the leadership of either the Head of House or Head of Year. Since these modules are much shorter than the average curricular unit it is much easier to test them and, as they are used by successive groups, so the material should become increasingly refined and enriched. The planning of such work by the team as a whole should concentrate their attention on common problems, while joint preparation of units by two or more tutors adds to the cohesiveness of the group.

One danger is that if such modules are 'banked' for use throughout the school, they may come to be used too frequently, pupils being faced with the same units time after time. Clear record-keeping, as suggested in Chapter 9, is one answer. Another is to develop 'stepped' or 'spiral' sets of modules which tackle the same problems at regular intervals, but in an increasingly sophisticated fashion as the pupils progress through the school.

Work on modules in the pastoral area cannot, of course, be divorced from that taking place within subject departments, especially those concerned with social, religious and behavioural issues. Any planning of modules in the area of, say, the individual and society must really be made with reference to the syllabuses of Sociology or Social Studies where it is quite possible that identical work is going on. Pastoral developments in the area of personal relationships or sex education need to complement approaches in Biology or Religious Studies; better still, they should be planned in conjunction with these departments. Units on money matters must involve Economics or Business Studies, while – as has been seen – study skills require liaison across the curriculum as a whole.

Cores and effect

All the factors outlined in this chapter need to be considered in the construction of a core curriculum for the lower part of the secondary school. The way in which modular planning can assist here, both in the structuring and development of experience, is exemplified in the work of Wantage School (Case Study Six).

CASE STUDY SIX
The Core Curriculum and its Extension at Wantage School, Oxfordshire.

The Third Year curriculum is based on a 50-hour fortnightly timetable, and consists of two main parts: the *Core* and *Extensions* to this.

40 hours are spent per fortnight on the *Core*, comprising:

- Mathematics
- English
- Tutorial
- PE/Games
- Sciences
- Modern Languages
- Humanities
- Creative/Art/Craft/Design

Within most subjects a degree of modular choice is available and each discipline '*extends*' the curriculum through optional units, each of which lasts for 12 or 13 weeks at five hours per fortnight. Pupils study two of these at any one time to make up their 50 hours. Other areas of study not included in the core also appear here:

- Child development
- Drama
- Geography
- History
- Home Economics
- Information technology
- Latin
- Music
- Religious Studies
- Textiles

Through these, pupils may broaden their programmes.

A total of *five* modules constitute a *GCSE* syllabus and in years Three to Five it is possible to programme 16 such units:

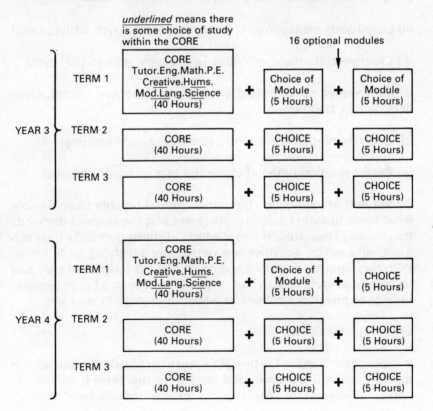

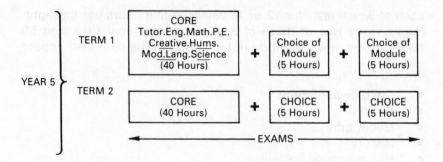

Details of the Physical Education syllabus illustrate the principles involved.

Physical Education

Core Curriculum All pupils will study physical education for 4 hours per fortnight, in which they will receive a balanced curriculum covering various aspects of the subject. These will include:

(a) Skilful body management (swimming, formal gym, athletics etc.)

(b) Creative and artistic activities (e.g. dance, educational gym)

(c) Competitive activities (e.g. soccer, rugby, hockey, cricket, rounders, tennis, badminton)

(d) Body training (cross country running, weight training)

(e) Personal environmental challenge (e.g. outdoor pursuits)

By the end of year three, the pupils should be able to appreciate what kinds of sports activities there are and the kinds of demands they make. They should know which of these demands they can meet, and which activities are personally satisfying or fulfilling. With this improved understanding of basic principles of play and technique in various activities, the pupil will be in a better position to choose physical activities in which to engage in later life.

Extending the CORE

It is possible to study for the GCSE exam in physical education, or just to take individual modules lasting for one term if they are of particular interest. In year three the extensions will be:

(i) Racquets extension – an interest course on the principles of play and basic techniques of racquet games such as badminton and tennis.

(ii) Health related fitness extension – an interest course involving fitness testing, circuit training, weight training and running training.

(iii) Sports extension – an interest course on the basic principles and techniques of aerobics, table tennis and handball.

(iv) Summer games extension (GCSE) – a course with a theory and practical element on athletics, swimming, and cricket/softball/rounders. This is part of the GCSE course in physical education; four further modules will need to be taken in years four and five.

Reproduced with permission from *Wantage School Third Year Choices* 1986/7

Upper school cores

In the upper part of the secondary school, a contrasting approach in the relationship between core and modules is presented by Ysgol Emrys ap Iwan (see Case Study Seven). Here the two are developed concurrently rather than consecutively, the timetable being blocked to ensure nine-week in-depth treatment of modules that have been selected.

CASE STUDY SEVEN
Core and Optional Modules at Ysgol Emrys ap Iwan

Each module is taught in two full afternoon blocks (two triple lessons) per week for nine weeks; that is $2 \times 3 \times 9 = 54$ lessons. Four afternoon blocks are set aside each week to permit two modules to be studied weekly. This would enable a pupil during the fourth and fifth year to study a total of 14 modules per year (8 in Form 4 and 6 in Form 5) from a list of 35 additional units on offer, although this list may vary depending upon demand.

	MONDAY	TUESDAY	WEDNESDAY	THURSDAY	FRIDAY
a.m.	Core	Core	Core	Core	Core
p.m.	Module 1	Module 1	Core	Module 2	Module 2

Each module is of approximately 40 hours' duration. It contains its own set of aims, objectives or short-term goals, learning outcomes, course content and learning experiences, performance criteria, learning strategies and assessment procedures. Assessment of a pupil's cumulative attainment is based upon performance criteria which are specified for each module. These describe the different levels of intended learning outcomes.

In many instances a system of 'Can-do' criteria-referenced profiles is used for this purpose, and these allow for formative and summative assessment. There is some danger of over-assessment (notably in terms of utilising teacher time) especially as the 'can-do' profiles and records of achievement are assessment tools. To be effective, these procedures need careful monitoring.

Curriculum Chart Years Four and Five

CORE STUDIES

ENGLISH		COMMUNICATIONS
Language	AND	French or German or Welsh or
Literature		Business Systems or Computing

MATHEMATICS

SCIENCE		TECHNOLOGY	
Biological Science or		Control Technology or	
General Science or		Craft Design Technology	or
Physical Science	AND	Media Systems	or
		Food & Home Technology	or
		Biological Science	

HUMAN STUDIES
Economics or Geography or History or Commerce

RELIGIOUS EDUCATION

ADDITIONAL STUDIES	
Art	Drama
Biological Science	Electronics
Calculus	Electronic Music
Child Care & Home Management*	Experience of Work
Community Relations	Food Preparation for Catering*
Computers in Business	French
Computer Control	Home Gardening
Computer Graphics	Home Maintenance
Computer Programming	Information Systems

Interview Techniques	Practical Office Skills
Introductory Computing	Psychology
Leisure	Robotics
Looking After Yourself	Technical Graphic Art
Mass Media	Tourism
Motor Vehicle Studies*	TV Production
Music	Typewriting
Personal Grooming & First Aid*	Welsh
Photography	Word Processing

*Taught in the Fifth year at Llandrillo Technical College

PLUS other modules as required

Reproduced with permission from S Pyart *Modules in Action: A School's Experience and Evaluation of a Modular Curriculum* Ysgol Emrys ap Iwan, Abergele

Within the academic sixth form, modularity is most frequently arrived at as a by-product of specialisation and an eagerness on the part of the staff to teach at this level. A course is normally shared out between members of the department, who then take responsibility for that specific section of it.

Some rationalisation of this curricular area is heralded by the GCE Boards' *Common Cores at Advanced Level*, which makes the modular approach feasible within a large institution, such as a sixth form or tertiary college, and most attractive on a consortia basis. With varying degrees of reluctance, the different boards put forward what they regarded as the areas most frequently covered within examination syllabuses at this level. On this basis, the 'core' of Economics, for example, would appear to be as described in Curricular Item 8.

CURRICULAR ITEM 8
The 'Core' of A Level Economics

A STATEMENT OF TOPICS COMMON TO THE A-LEVEL ECONOMICS SYLLABUSES OF ALL BOARDS*

1. THE CENTRAL PROBLEM OF ECONOMIC SOCIETIES

Scarcity, choice and allocation of resources; the market mechanism. Private and public goods.

2.   **THEORY OF DEMAND**

Consumer behaviour; the derivation of individual and market demand curves; price, income and cross-elasticities of demand. Total and marginal utility; income and substitution effects; consumers' surplus; joint demand; shifts in the demand schedule.

3.   **THEORY OF SUPPLY**

Behaviour of firms; the derivation of firm and industry supply curves; elasticity of supply. The short run; the law of variable proportions. The long run; economies and diseconomies of scale. Total, average and marginal costs.

4.   **PRICE AND OUTPUT DETERMINATION**

The interaction of supply and demand; different market structures, price and output determination under perfect competition, imperfect competition including oligopoly, monopoly. Total, average and marginal revenues. Equilibrium of the firm and the industry in the short and long run.

5.   **THEORY OF DISTRIBUTION**

Demand for and supply of factors of production. The determination of wages, interest, profits, rents and quasi-rent. The role of trade unions.

6.   **NATIONAL INCOME ACCOUNTING**

The definition and measurement of income, expenditure and output; net and gross; national and domestic; market prices and factor cost. Relationship between measures. Problems of comparison over time and between countries.

7.   **THEORY OF INCOME DETERMINATION**

The circular flow of income, injections into the flow (investment, government expenditure, exports) and withdrawals from it (saving, taxes, imports). The consumption function. The multiplier. The aceleration principle. The equilibrium level of income. Inflationary and deflationary gaps.

8. MONEY, PRICES AND BANKING

The nature and functions of money and credit. The demand for and supply of money. Definition and measurement of changes in the value of money. The money market, functions of the Bank of England and commercial banks; reserve ratios. The operation of monetary policy: interest rates, open market operations, special deposits. Causes and effects of changes and rates of change in the price level.

9. INTERNATIONAL TRADE

The gains from trade. The principle of comparative costs. Free trade and protection. Fixed and flexible exchange rates. The International Monetary Fund and present international monetary arrangements. The terms of trade. The United Kingdom balance of payments: current account and capital account.

10. THE ROLE OF THE GOVERNMENT

Public provision and distribution of goods and services. The distinction between private and social costs. The management of the national, regional and local economies. Policy instruments for influencing the rate of growth of output, the level of employment, the price level, the distribution of income and wealth and the balance of payments. Direct controls, fiscal and monetary policies, the regulation of prices and incomes. Measures to influence the location of industry and the distribution of employment. The regulation of monopolies and restrictive practices. Nationalised industries.

*It should be noted that the specifications may vary in form amongst the Boards, and that in some syllabuses they may be included by implication rather than as distinct statements.

Reproduced with permission from *Common Cores at Advanced Level* GCE Boards of England, Wales and Northern Ireland, 1983 pp 24,25

As will be seen in the next Chapter, A/S Level proposals and the development of pre-vocational education are doing even more to modify the traditional curriculum and conventional approaches at this level.

For further reading

Two basic books on the core curriculum are: *Towards a Compulsory Curriculum* (1973) by J P White and *The Common Curriculum* (1979) by M Holt, both published by Routledge and Kegan Paul.

The idea of a primary school 'core' is suggested by HMI in *Primary Schools In England* (HMSO, 1978). The developments leading up to and incorporating this are traced in J Stewart's *The Making of the Primary School* (Open University Press, 1985), R L Lowe's *The Changing Primary School* (Falmer Press, 1987) and R J Campbell's *Developing the Primary School Curriculum* (Holt Saunders, 1985). More flexible approaches are described in D Hamilton's *In Search of Structure* (Hodder & Stoughton, 1981), J O Greig and J C Brown's *Activity Methods in the Middle Years* (Oliver and Boyd, 1975) and A Hargreaves' *Two Cultures of Schooling: the Case of Middle Schools* (Falmer Press, 1986). Important research findings at this level form the basis of the ILEA's *Junior School Project* (1985), N Bennett and C Desforges' *The Quality of Public Learning Experiences* (Lawrence Erlbaum Associates, 1986) and of *Progress and Performance in the Primary Classroom* (Routledge and Kegan Paul, 1980).

In *Aspects of Secondary Education* (HMSO, 1979) and *Curriculum 11–16* (HMSO, 1977), the HMI cast a critical eye on such developments, putting foward suggestions for reform which they later amplified in *A View of the Curriculum* (HMSO, 1980) and *Curriculum 11–16: A Review of Progress* (HMSO, 1981). The DES' view appeared in *A Framework for the School Curriculum* (1980), but for a more recent analysis see HMI's *The Curriculum from 5 to 16* (HMSO, 1985), the more subject-related booklets in the *Curriculum Matters* series, and *Better Schools* (HMSO, 1985). The work of Ysgol Emrys ap Iwan, referred to in this chapter, is given in greater detail in *Modules in Action: A School's Experience* by S Pyart, available from the school. See also *An Approach to Learning – Beliefs and aims; The Open Curriculum* (Deeside Community College, Clwyd, 1974–86).

Several books are currently available relating to study skills, including *Teaching Information Skills at Primary Level*, edited by P Avann (Edward Arnold, 1985), *Teaching Study Skills* by D Hamblin (Basil Blackwell, 1981) and *Study and Information skills Across the Curriculum* by A Irving (Heinemann, 1983).

4 Options, Community and Pre-Vocational Issues

If the kind of groundwork suggested in the last chapter has been laid in the lower part of the school, the stage will be set for the introduction of successful modular options at the beginning of the fourth year. Here, as *Better Schools* says,

> A difficult balance has to be struck between accommodating pupils' special interests and aptitudes, and retaining breadth and balance so that no pupil can drop subjects or other elements whose continued study may be an essential foundation for subsequent learning, training or work.[1]

The common core will therefore need to continue and in most schools is likely to take the form of compulsory key modules. These have the purpose of linking all the work being done, broadening out specialist choices and providing the 'essential elements' referred to above.

Refining choice

The overriding problems at this stage concern the scale of the operation – options selected from within different combinations of subject blockings seldom entirely match individual student need – and the finality of such decisions. There is little chance of turning back or changing direction once option schemes have got underway!

Modules, on the other hand, being conceived on a much smaller scale, and having their objectives precisely spelt out, are infinitely more flexible. They serve a multitude of purposes and can be combined to meet almost any need. New modules may be added and old ones discarded in direct response to changing demand. The direction and nature of the programme may be altered, or modules re-taken, as required. Nor need the modular contribution come from one area of the curriculum alone. Important

---

[1]   DES *Better Schools* HMSO, 1985, para 68

dimensions of a subject, often neglected because they fall within the province of another discipline, can now be incorporated with comparative ease, or complementary modules followed to provide additional insight into work of a highly specialist nature.

Reforming the system

Modules will, of course, have to be carefully planned if they are not merely to duplicate the weaknesses revealed in the system by the 1979 national survey, *Aspects of Secondary Education*. This wrote of options as

> building blocks, some with a fine patina of tradition, some still comparatively novel, with very few rules governing their selection and assembly.[2]

It can easily be imagined how a fragmented curriculum such as this could become positively kaleidoscopic were insufficient attention paid to the finer details – something that becomes possible once planning is focused on these smaller units of work.

The stress laid upon objectives, spelt out in precise terms, facilitates a selection of modules that corresponds closely to individual need and accords well with the criteria-referencing of GCSE. Such objectives will cover not only content, level and – if appropriate – direct relationship with other units, but also method of approach. The influence of external examinations resulted, according to the 1979 *Survey*, in

> . . . heavily directed teaching, a preponderance of dictated or copied notes, an emphasis on the giving and recall of information, with little room or time for enquiry or exploration of applications.[3]

It is doubtful whether such outcomes could arise among modules such as those described here, available to all on the open market. Still less would doubt be expressed as to

> whether energies are being effectively harnessed, and whether the pupils are gaining sufficient experience of ordering their own effort.[4]

The way in which all this works out in practice can be seen within the Science and Technology Department of Peers School, Oxford (Case Study Eight).

---

[2] HMI *Aspects of Secondary Education* HMSO, 1979, p266
[3] *Ibid* p 262
[4] *Ibid*

CASE STUDY EIGHT
Modular Options in Science and Technology

It will be seen that a series of units on *Biology, Geology, Physics, Design, Technology and Chemistry* may be combined in a variety of ways, according to the specialisation required. Students may be prepared for the new, differentiated *GCSE* examination through a selection of modules which provide an appropriate amount of content for the level at which they are aiming. At the same time, they have the opportunity of seeing the inter-relationship of other approaches through choosing to follow units in adjacent areas of interest. The generalist will have the chance to select modules across the full range offered and thus gain a good overview of this area of the curriculum. The modular scheme in this format also provides for the late developer and the slow learner by delaying decisions regarding the level at which the examination will be taken, or whether an individual sits for it at all, until well on into the course. There is also the benefit of a variety of teaching styles and approaches to be considered.

SA1		SB1		SC1			SA2		SB2	
B31	Microbes	T16	Health Science	B35	Body Maintenance		B35	Body Maintenance	T16	Health Science
G31	Minerals	P31	Energy Resources	G32	Astronomy		T15	Earth Science	P31	Energy Resources
BO1	Feeding	BO1	Feeding	B31	Microbes		BO2	Respiration + Homeostasis	BO2	Respiration + Homeostasis
P33	Microelectronics	T10	Basic Technology	PO1	Physics of Movement		P33	Microelectronics	T11	Practical Electronics
D38	Jewellery	D38	Jewellery	D38	Jewellery		D34	Woodcraft	D38	Jewellery
T18	Graphics	T18	Graphics	T18	Graphics		D32	Materials	D32	Materials
D34	Woodwork	D34	Woodwork	D34	Woodwork		D39	Design	D39	Design
T10	Basic Technology	PO1	Physics of Movement	B34	Food Science Technology		T11	Practical Electricity	PO2	Molecule Picture of Matter
C31	Dyes & Dyeing	N32	Fibres & Fabrics	CO1	Elements & Compounds		C31	Dyes + Dyeing	N32	Fibres & Fabrics
B23	Social Biology	B31	Microbes	BO1	Feeding Relationships		B23	Social Biology	B23	Social Biology
PO1	Physics of Movement	N31	Textile Technology	N31	Textile Technology		PO2	Molecule Picture of Matter	N31	Textile Technology
T16	Health Science	C32	Science of Crime Detection	B51	Our Health		T16	Health Science	C32	Science of Crime Detection
P35	Gears & Gearing	P32	Domestic Electricity	P33	Microelectronics		P35	Gears & Gearing	P32	Domestic Electricity
CO1	Elements & Compounds	C35	Photography	C35	Photography		CO2	Properties & Structure of Matter	C35	Photography

Reproduced with permission from Peers School, Oxford

Multiple outcomes

The Community Studies Department at the same school (Peers, Oxford) has adapted a somewhat different approach to enable an even greater variety of examination and non-examination courses to emerge from a common set of modules (*Case Study Nine*).

CASE STUDY NINE
Modular Options in Community Studies

Various student needs have been identified here – those wishing to take GCSE, those who are following a TVEI course and those for whom a more integrated *Humanities* programme would be more appropriate. Modules are available in this last broad area having titles such as *Pollution and Conservation, People and Power, Consumer Affairs* etc . . . Those wishing to follow the *Humanities* programme must choose a central core of these, namely: *People and Work, Prejudice* and *Beliefs*. All GCSE students must choose at least one module from this list, the others being selected from the specialist options, that is, modules grouped under subject headings – *Religious Studies, Needlecraft and Textiles, History, Geography, Environmental Studies, Home Economics, Community, Catering Studies*. TVEI students follow the GCSE pattern, but in addition take two modules from the general titles, on *Community* and the *Mass Media*. In addition to this, a personal profile on *Health and Fitness* is drawn up for each individual.

Reproduced with permission from Peers School, Oxford

General studies

General Studies can play an important part in broadening and deepening academic study at sixth form level – or, indeed, at any stage within the system. Once again, the general principle underlying such modules should be that they are short-term, free-standing units which are open to all, and have objectives and content that are clearly expressed.

Case Study Ten focuses on a sixth-form college, and explains what can be achieved in this way.

CASE STUDY TEN
The Use of General Study Modules at Farnham College, Surrey

The curriculum at Farnham College consists of a large number of separate subjects. These can be studied at any level, either towards an examination or for their own individual worth. Of course, the first of these functions does not preclude the second, nor should the second rule out the first!

It is your responsibility, assisted by your tutor and the subject staff, to make a sensible and informed selection from all the subjects that are on offer. Here, the career you hope to follow, success or enjoyment in various subjects in the Fourth and Fifth Year, the requirements of higher education or entry to a specific trade or profession may well be uppermost in your mind.

Together with these subjects Farnham College offers a wide range of shorter courses which go alongside them and enable you, again taking your tutor's advice, to build an interesting and varied programme . . .

General study modules are one-term courses on which may be used to add to, complement or develop your personal skills, knowledge or interests. They are really very much what you make of them. If you take little trouble or time in considering which are the most appropriate for you; if you fail to take what advice is available concerning them; if you regard them as something imposed from above – then you are likely to find General Studies somewhat tedious and primarily you have yourself to blame!

If, however, you make some time available and take some effort in selecting wisely from the list which follows, they can enhance the rest of your studies enormously.

Checklist for choice
a Read the description of each General Study carefully, even those in which you think you have little interest. You never know what you may find!
b Seek the advice of your tutor, senior tutor, subject staff or others who have followed the course.
c Consider the basis on which you will make this choice. Will it be:
  i To complement, or add to your knowledge, of an exam subject?
  ii To link two or more subjects?
  iii To assist in the development of an interest, hobby or skill?
  iv To lay the groundwork of new interests, hobbies or skills?
  v To begin an entirely new area of study which appeals to you?
  vi To broaden your interests across the full range of human experience. (The General Studies are classified under five broad headings to help you do this if you wish.)
d If you find it impossible to obtain an interesting General Study during one of your available periods, remember that Community Service covers a vast range of activities both on site and off. Each term all General Studies are re-timetabled and you may find the new times more convenient.
e Attend the General Studies Circus early to sign up and thus avoid disappointment.

f   Regular attendance at General Studies is, of course, required once you have signed up for them. See the Director of Curriculum if there are good reasons for wanting to change a General Study once you have joined it.
g   Once you have made your selection do not lose this information sheet. You will need to refer to it when making your choices for the Spring and Summer terms and it will not be re-printed.
h   Let the Director of Curriculum or your tutor know if you feel that any particular General Study should be included in this programme or if you would like to run a General Study yourself (last year two of the most successful General Studies – *Dungeons and Dragons* and *Modern Dance* – were run entirely by students.

Assessment
Although most General Studies are non-examinable courses, you will be expected to offer or produce at least one assessable contribution to each you attend (eg the introduction of a topic for discussion, written work produced during one of your timetabled periods, production of a piece of pottery, etc). Staff will explain in the first session of each course what the particular contribution to that course will be. When General Studies are reported on, Credits will be given for satisfactory participation in the course concerned. This information may well be used in writing references for testimonials.

Reproduced with permission from Farnham College, Surrey

Broadening 'A' level work

More formal moves than this are currently under consideration regarding such a broadening out of the sixth form curriculum through the examination system. Modules play a large part in the new *AS Level* proposals.

These new courses are designed to cover about half the material of a traditional A level subject over a two-year period, with special emphasis upon practical application. The DES have produced figures indicative of the narrow concentration upon one specific area of the curriculum by students leaving our schools. They would therefore:

> like as many students specializing in Science and Mathematics as possible to continue during their A level years the systematic study of, for example, English, History or a Foreign Language; and as many students specializing in the Arts and Humanities as possible to continue the systematic study of, for example, Mathematics, Technology or one of the Sciences.[5]

[5]   DES *AS Levels* HMSO, 1984 para 7

The combination of 'A' and 'AS' level work envisaged under these proposals would be both facilitated and enriched through the kind of modular approach outlined above, with the DES reiterating its stress that:

> *contrasting* 'AS' levels – say, English for science students or mathematics for humanities students – will be of particular value in broadening studies. *Complementary* AS levels – say, design and technology for science students – will also offer opportunities for broadening a chosen area of study.[6]

The wider community

Reference has already been made to the use of modules in linking the school with the wider community it serves. This is relevant to every stage within the system, but the introduction of pre-vocational courses such as CPVE, CGLI and TVEI makes it particularly appropriate in the upper levels of secondary schools and within colleges.

This need for a closer relationship between what goes on in a school and the requirements of the wider society beyond its gates featured prominently in Section Two of *Curriculum 11–16*, but found its clearest expression in the pages of the *Taylor Report*, which claimed:

> A school is not an end in itself; it is an institution set up and financed by society to achieve certain objectives which society regards as desirable and it is subject to all the stresses to which society itself is subject. It is vital, therefore, that teachers have the support of people outside the school in the increasingly difficult task of attaining those objectives and dealing with those stresses.[7]

Taylor's influential findings centred upon a 'new partnership' in the governance of schools, consisting of staff, parents, LEA, local community and – in some cases – the pupils themselves.

Parallel with this is the idea of education as a life-long process, with the school as a focal point throughout. Certainly, the *Coventry Working Party* (see p 15) see modular planning as one of the keys to such developments, which will require:

> the development of provision for all adults to join in informal and formal ways at various levels, times and stages in life: when, where, how and what the individual need. This is in contrast with the present system which can be likened to a steam railway: you can only progress on the education gravy train if you get on the right train at the right time and with the right ticket(s). We need to break away from such a rigid delivery system of fixed

---

6 DES *Broadening A Level Studies: A Guide for Schools and Colleges*, HMSO, 1986
7 *A New Partnership for Our Schools* The Taylor Report, HMSO, 1977

entry points, of hours in a day, terms, academic years and self-contained levels and entry qualifications.

This open access to education throughout life will require:

i   development of the existing provision of higher education, further education, and adult/community education.
ii a system of modules or credits which are inter-changeable between levels and systems including the recognition of the less formal and non-vocational provision.
iii distance learning and support systems
iv cultural and community group provision.
v   more mixed age groups in the learning activity situation.

Fortunately the technology is now becoming available to enable this. No longer is it essential (or always efficient) to gather learners together in an institution to receive their education from a knowledgeable teacher. The knowledge can be developed through inter-active processes using tv, computers, video and disc materials at home or at a distance.[8]

In the mid-1970s the wider community outside the school, especially its commercial aspects, found an equally compelling voice – that of James Callaghan. His Ruskin speech of October, 1976,[9] focused national attention on a range of governmental concerns. Notable among these was the involvement of industry, commerce and local employers in the way our schools were run and what was taught within them. The 'Great Debate' was underway!

This increased accountability of schools has been a major theme since the mid-1970s, exemplified in a number of small, yet significant, developments – the publication of HMI Reports; the 1980 Act's mandate that a school's aims and examination results must appear in the prospectus; the emergence of the Assessment of Performance Unit (APU); the demise of the Schools Council; the emergence of the Secondary Examinations Council (SEC); and continuing governmental pressure for the extension of governing bodies and an increase in their powers.

Modular flexibility facilitates the kind of approach envisaged within the developments outlined above. This allows units of work lasting a matter of weeks only, to be developed, coupled with an appropriate blocking of the timetable to enable this to occur. One of the main advantages of such a system is that it permits significant periods of time to be spent on work outside the classroom, without the whole of the curriculum being distorted to accommodate such endeavours. Similarly, it enables those working within the local community to make a contribution to

---

8   Coventry Education Committee *Comprehensive Education for Life* 1984, p.46
9   See DES/Welsh Office *Schools in England and Wales. Current Issues: an Annotated Agenda for Discussion* HMSO, 1976

what is going on inside a school, without calling for an unreasonable commitment of their time or resources. The clarity of the objectives helps the layman to appreciate precisely what is required of him, as well as enabling those outside the school to take an active part in this whole process of objective-setting.

Schemes such as these can be slotted in or out of the curriculum at relatively short notice. They can also form valuable additions to either a compulsory core or optional modules at any level. Their inclusion on a profile or certificate of unitary accreditation (see p. 204) cannot but be helpful to the school leaver seeking employment, and such links with the local community are a common feature in many GCSE syllabuses. Rather than tackling them separately in each Department, a school would do well to adopt a common modular approach to their timetabling.

A good example of what can be achieved through such links is provided in Case Study Eleven.

CASE STUDY ELEVEN
Modular Linkage with Industry,
St Kentigern's Academy, West Lothian, Scotland

THE INDUSTRIAL STUDIES COURSE

This consists of 4 units:

Unit 1 What is Industry?
Unit 2 Industrial Relations?
Unit 3 Life after School
Unit 4 Computer Studies

The course is taught to mixed ability 4th year classes. There are 8 classes, with approximately 15 pupils in each, and pupils spend 3 periods a week on Industrial Studies, one double and one single period. Eight teachers are involved from a wide subject area which has included: Business Studies, Geography, Modern Studies, Science, Maths, Home Economics and History. Not only does this prevent the course becoming the province of one particular department but it is also in keeping with a basic aim of the Education for the Industrial Society Project, that of pervading and permeating the existing curriculum.

Each teacher specialises in a particular unit and classes rotate among the teachers every 10 weeks. This means that by the end of the school year every class will have covered the 4 units.

At first sight the course may seem over-ambitious, bearing in mind *a* the time limit of one year; *b* the apparent complexity of some of the content. However, the course has been designed with mixed ability pupils in mind and has been refined in terms of presentation to such a degree that it is not only easily digested, but can be covered in the time available.

The course is backed up by a Central Resources Base which is stocked with video-tapes, audio-tapes, slides, various game kits, overhead transparencies, worksheets, etc. The teaching approach is 'dynamic' in the sense that pupils are encouraged to get involved in role-play, simulations, discussions, problem-solving and practical experience of computer technology.

PUPILS CHANGE UNIT EVERY 10 WEEKS.

UNIT I: THE ROLE OF INDUSTRY

Industry creates our national wealth and contributes to our standard of living. Manufacturing industry alone accounts for half of our total exports and is responsible directly for a third of total employment.

It is essential therefore that pupils are aware of the central role Industry plays in our society, and while this course unit deals mainly with manufacturing industry it is not confined to it.

1 *What is Industry?*   Industry can be broken down into 3 categories: Primary, Secondary and Tertiary. Sample studies are made from each category and the inter-relationships within Industry are stressed.

2 *How Industry Works*   It is important that pupils are able to understand the nature of industry and how it works. Special case studies are made of the steel and car industries and these highlight such things as hierarchy of management, boardroom decisions, the workings of a production line, life on the shop floor and the basic structure of a firm. Examples from local factories are extensively used and this section is backed up with visits to local industry.

3 *Location of Industry*   Particular attention is focused here on the new town of Livingston and the work of the Livingston Development Corporation in attracting new industry. Essential factors in the decision to locate a new factory include: raw materials, transport, labour, capital, site, market, power and the role of Government. Two particular areas emphasised are labour and the role of Government.

All the factors that determine the location of a factory are brought together in an examination of the impact of a new factory on all aspects of the community.

4 *Closure*   This section looks at some of the causes of factories closing down eg industrial relations problems, poor management, product suitability, Government role and the state of the economy etc.

The importance of Industry is again stressed with a brief study of the effects of closure upon the community and how these effects go further than those simply made redundant.

INDUSTRIAL VISITS

Each week two groups of 15 pupils from Industrial Studies classes are taken on an industrial visit. The timetable is so arranged as to allow a ninth teacher to brief the pupils in a single period before the visit, and to spend a double period (larger if necessary) with the pupils on the visit. Follow-up work is done by the class teacher at the next Industrial Studies class. At the end of each term every pupil will have been out on at least one visit. Essential for the working of the industrial visits has been a permanent booking of the school mini-bus by the Industrial Studies Programme.

Although the visits are heavily tied in to the course they are not necessarily confined to it and a wide range of locations are visited which fit in with the broad aims of Education for the Industrial Society.

Golden Wonder Crisps, Broxburn	Pupils see production line in operation in modern factory
Woolco Store, Livingston	Good example of a Tertiary Industry. Tied in to units (1) and (2)
Royal Bank of Scotland Training Centre	Tied in to all four units eg examples of modern computer technology applications and the emphasis the Royal Bank puts on Industrial Relations
Marks, Polbeth	Produces clothes for Marks and Spencer. Inter-relationship of industry stressed here

Reproduced with permission from St Kentigern's Academy, *Industrial Studies Programme* pp 1–3, 1.

Pre-vocational education

The sophisticated use of *Introductory*, *Exploratory* and *Preparatory* modules within CPVE has already been noted (p. 31) as have TVEI schemes, which seek to integrate work of this kind within the everyday curriculum of a school. These schemes are conducted within guidelines established by the MSC, which state that such approaches must:

- provide equality of opportunity for both sexes
- consist of a four-year curriculum suitable for adult life in a rapidly changing world
- place emphasis upon active learning and personal development
- blend vocational with more general education
- relate to local employment prospects
- contain carefully planned work experience
- link up with educational opportunities available at a later stage
- contain valid assessment procedures

- take place alongside the preparation for other examinations
- follow a competently conducted pilot scheme

Types of curricular pattern to emerge within such schemes include:

1 The selection of *options* alongside those already offered, either linked to, blocked alongside them or free standing;
2 The development of pre-vocational *elements* within a *common core*;
3 Focusing upon a *theme* which incorporates a specific set of options;
4 Running an *integrated course* spanning the option blocks;
5 Establishing a common programme consisting of *taster units* taken by all students as a prelude to further specialisation at a later stage (see p. 13).

Such schemes are outlined in *TVEI Review 1985* which explains how each one

> may be designed on a modular basis; that is, with short units of learning, allowing students to select different combinations of units and to build up a personal programme over the first two years to meet their individual needs[10]

Just what can be achieved when such an approach is adopted by a consortium of schools is illustrated in Case Study Twelve.

CASE STUDY TWELVE
The Use of Modules in Coventry's TVEI Programme

THE COVENTRY TVEI PROJECT
In common with all other projects Coventry will have some 200–250 fourteen-year old young people entering the scheme in each of four years.

The participating institutions are:

Finham Park

Foxford

Woodway Park

Henley College of Further Education

It is proposed that all non-TVEI secondary schools should have opportunity to associate with the project at a variety of levels. This will range from formal links between TVEI and non-TVEI

[10] MSC *TVEI Review 1985*

schools to informal curriculum discussion and access to TVEI sponsored in-service training.

The curriculum in schools during years 1 and 2 of the scheme consists of:

a   an inner core, not exclusive to TVEI, but within which subject content will be enhanced to recognise the contribution of TVEI to the general curriculum. The inner core will include English, Mathematics, Science, Humanities, PE and expressive experience, personal development and guidance.
b   an outer core of TVEI modules
c   TVEI linked options;
d   a general options scheme shared with the rest of the school, an important feature of which is the opportunity to take a foreign language.

Most of these options are either new to the schools or have been enhanced.

The Modular Approach

A modular approach has been chosen within TVEI because it facilitates a rapid response to curriculum change and allows for breadth, balance and relevance. Students are able to negotiate their own routes through modules which are given coherence by 'clustering'. There is some evidence that students favour a modular approach because the learning objectives are short-term and the scheme allows for variety. The use of half-day sessions for modules gives opportunity for a variety of learning approaches to be taken some of them off-site. Potentially the modular scheme allows for mixed-age provision offering greater organisational flexibility.

Essential features of the Coventry project

(i)   *Residential Experience*
Each TVEI student will have the benefit of a residential experience once during the four year course. A feature of this experience is that students will actively participate in deciding the nature and organisation of the residential experience. This will probably operate through the structure of the student's course tutor group.

CURRICULUM STRUCTURE 14–16. COVENTRY TVEI PROJECT

CURRICULUM STRUCTURE	CURRICULUM DESCRIPTION	PROPORTION OF SCHOOL WEEK	
CORE — INNER: GENERAL	ENGLISH MATHEMATICS PE/EXPRESSIVE STUDIES HUMANITIES SCIENCE PERSONAL DEVELOPMENT/GUIDANCE	60%	CAREERS GUIDANCE
CORE — OUTER: TVEI MODULAR COURSE	STUDENTS FOLLOW TWO MODULES FOR EACH NINE WEEK PERIOD. THE MODULES WILL OPERATE ON TWO HALF DAYS EACH WEEK SO THAT EACH STUDENT CAN COMPLETE FOURTEEN MODULES OVER THE COURSE OF TWO YEARS. (a) ADVERTISING & MARKETING (k) MODERN BUSINESS SYSTEMS (2) (b) BIOTECHNOLOGY (l) MODERN OFFICE PRACTICE (c) COMPUTER LITERACY (4) (m) PHOTOGRAPHY (d) CONTROL TECHNOLOGY (4) (n) PRODUCT DEVELOPMENT (e) FOOD & RELATED SERVICES (o) SERVICES IN THE COMMUNITY (2) (f) FOOD TECHNOLOGY (p) TECHNICAL GRAPHICS (g) GRAPHIC DESIGN (q) TEXTILE DESIGN (h) INFORMATION PROCESSING (r) THE FASHION INDUSTRY (i) MASS MEDIA (2) (s) UNDERSTANDING BRITISH IND. (4) (j) MICROELECTRONICS (4) (t) WORD PROCESSING NB. THE NUMBERS IN BRACKETS REFER TO THE NUMBER OF SUB MODULES AVAILABLE UNDER THE TITLE OF THAT MODULE.	20%	RESIDENTIAL EXPERIENCE
OPTIONS — TVEI LINKED	EACH STUDENT WILL CHOOSE ONE OPTION FROM AMONG THE FOLLOWING: ART AND CRAFT HOME ECONOMICS/FOOD INDUSTRY BUSINESS STUDIES TECHNOLOGY CDT TEXTILES AND FASHION DANCE AND DRAMA TYPEWRITING/OFFICE PRACTICE	10%	WORK EXPERIENCE
OPTIONS — GENERAL	EACH STUDENT WILL CHOOSE ONE OPTION HUMANITIES MUSIC MODERN LANGUAGES SCIENCE	10%	

TVEI: MODULAR CLUSTERS FOR ACCREDITATION

The assessment of each candidate will be carried out by teachers in the centre. Each candidate may study up to two packages of five modules and will be assessed on the work completed in each of these modules. Students will select modules progressively. Counselling during the course will lead them to compose *one or two* of the packages outlined below. Guidance will aim to support vocational options and to balance them.

Each package or cluster = 5 modules = 1 subject.

Options:

Studies in British Industry
Computer Literacy 1 or Product Development
Two modules from Understanding British Industry (4)
A further two from   : Understanding British Industry (4)
                  : Information Processing
                  : Word Processing
                  : Advertising and Marketing
                  : The Fashion Industry

Modern Business Systems
Computer Literacy 1 or Product Development
Two modules from Modern Business Systems (2)
A further two from   : Information Processing
                  : Word Processing
                  : Modern Office Practice

Business Application
Computer Literacy 1 or Product Development
Two modules from Understanding British Industry (4)
A further two from   : Understanding British Industry (4)
                  : Modern Business Systems (2)
                  : Information Processing
                  : Word Processing
                  : Advertising and Marketing
                  : Modern Office Practice

Computer Literacy
Four Computer Literacy modules plus
One module from   : Microelectronics 1 or 2
                : Information Processing
                : Word Processing

Enterprise Technology
Computer Literacy 1 or Product Development
Two modules from Understanding British Industry (4)
A further two from   : Control Technology (4)
                  : Food Technology
                  : Biotechnology

Technological Studies
Computer Literacy 1 or Product Development
Three modules from Control Technology (4)
A further one from   : Other Control Technology
                : Microelectronics (4)
                : Technical Graphics
                : Food Technology
                : Biotechnology

Microelectronics and Control
Computer Literacy 1 or Product Development
Three modules from Microelectronics (4)
A further one from   : Control Technology (4)
                : Other Microelectronics module

Information Processing
Computer Literacy 1 or Product Development
Information Processing
A further three from : Computer Literacy Module
                 : Word Processing
                 : Technical Graphics
                 : Mass Media (2)

Media Studies
Computer Literacy 1 or Product Development
Mass Media 1
Graphic Design
A further two from   : Mass Media 2
                  : Advertising and Marketing
                  : Photography

Design Studies
Product Development
Graphic Design
Textile Design
The Fashion Industry
Photography

Services in the Community
Computer Literacy 1 or Product Development
Two modules from Services in the Community (2)
A further two from   : Food Technology
                  : Food and Related Services
                  : Biotechnology

Food Technology
Computer Literacy 1 or Product Development
Food Technology
Food and Related Services
A further two from   : Advertising and Marketing
                  : Photography
                  : Word Processing
                  : Modern Business Systems
                  : Biotechnology

B Disqualified combinations of clusters
The following combinations of modules are disallowed by the Examination Board:
(a) Studies in British Industry and Business Application
(b) Computer Literacy and Information Processing
(c) Enterprise Technology and Technological Studies
(d) Media Studies and Design Studies

*B The numbers in brackets refer to the number of sub-modules available under each modular title.

(ii) *Equal opportunities*
Coventry's TVEI schools recognise the need for positive action in order to attract more girls to TVEI courses and to encourage all pupils to make non-sex-stereotyped choices of courses. The TVEI modular curriculum structure combined with appropriate counselling techniques has shown some success in encouraging girls to opt for non-traditional courses. It is hoped that boys choices will show a similar trend in the future.

Coventry's TVEI schools also recognise the need to develop whole-school approaches to equal opportunities in order to tackle sex-stereotyped influences which lie beyond the TVEI curriculum. Two members of staff from each school, together with one member of staff from Henley College will meet regularly with the Teacher Adviser for Equal Opportunities (gender) to monitor girls' and boys' progress on TVEI courses and to share experiences of whole school strategies.

Working groups will be established within each school to research aspects of equal opportunities and pilot new approaches designed to counteract sex-stereotyping.

(iii) *Special Educational Needs*
Within the project there is provision for young people with wide ranging academic and social abilities. It is the intention that some special school students, whose needs might in part be met by a TVEI programme of work, should have access to the outer core modules.

(iv) *Profiling*
The adoption of a modular curriculum lends itself to the logical corollary of pupil profiling and the continuous assessment of achievement. Under the modular arrangements with blocked morning or afternoon sessions, the inclusion of practical work and experiential processes contribute to a continuing dialogue between teacher and pupil. The thrust of profiling in TVEI is on student participation and an agreed outcome between student and teacher.

(v) *Links with industry/work experience*
Planned work experience is an integral part of the TVEI programme. In conjunction with the Careers Service the TVEI schools and college are piloting a new approach to work experience and industrial links.

Employers will be informed about TVEI and in particular the experiences and qualifications students will achieve. It is intended to establish a register of work placement opportunities from which students will choose and make application. This scheme will actively involve employers and teachers in monitoring work experience placements opening up possible curriculum links between schools and industry.

(vi) *Evaluation*
The Evaluation of the Coventry TVEI project is being undertaken by Professor Eggleston and his curriculum team at Warwick University. The Evaluation of the project will be formative in nature so influencing the development of TVEI as it proceeds. A Coventry teacher has been seconded for a day a week to work as field officer assisting with the evaluation process in schools.

(vii)*Supported self-study*
Supported self-study is an attempt to provide students with learning resources and tutorial support that will enable them to learn and work more effectively and independently.

16–18 developments in TVEI
The 16–18 phase in TVEI is seen as a continuation of the process begun at 14 with students receiving an enhanced technical and vocational dimension to their general educatiion. It is essential that those processes of student/staff negotiation, active learning and personal development find practical expression in the 16–18 phase. The notion of teachers as facilitators and managers of learning increasingly needs to be developed so that students are more independent and self-disciplined. The curriculum framework 16–18 will consist of three major components:

(a) Main course of study
(b) Integrating and supportive study modules
(c) Core experiences including:
    Planned work experience
    Personal recording and profiling
    Counselling and Careers guidance
    Information Technology
    Product Development

Reproduced with permission from Coventry LEA *Technical and Vocational Education Initiative* 1986, pp 2, 4, 6, 8–10, 13

Vocational training

Some of the earliest and most successful uses of modular planning were developed within the area of vocational training. The *Technician Education Council* (TEC) developed standard modules of three kinds – essential, optional and complementary.[11] The *Business Education Council* (BEC) were more liberal in the way modules were combined but brought in an element of control through four unifying themes, relating to *money matters, interpersonal skills, communication* and *information technology*.[12] These courses have subsequently been amalgamated into *BTEC*, which achieves the balance – explored in Chapter Two – between coherence and diversity through:

> *Core Units*, or parts of grouped courses which are essential for all courses at a given level associated with a particular vocational area.
> *Core Skills*, which are identified for each course, but which always include the inter-personal and other general skills necessary for success in work.
> *Core Themes*, which are a means of relating core skills to course content.[13]

A BTEC unit normally lasts 60–90 hours and can be taken either full or part-time, at three levels: *First, National* and *Higher*.

In-service training

Possibly the most neglected of all modular possibilities lies in the field of management training and education. Certain quite specific skills are required at any level of management. All those in managerial positions are, for example, required to chair meetings, assess the work of those for whom they are responsible, conduct interviews, take decisions, use their time constructively, motivate those within their team, give professional counselling or guidance, and so on.

Most managerial courses last for several days and deal with the full range of such matters. Whilst it must be appreciated that all these aspects interrelate, it should nevertheless be possible to have available short, practical units which can be set up at short notice in direct response to individual need, as and when this occurs. This could be organised, for instance, by a consortium of schools, either on one another's premises or at the local teachers' centre. As few as three or four members of staff, but not more than, say, a dozen could attend each module.

---

[11]   Technician Education Council *Policy Statement* TEC, 1974
[12]   Business Education Council *First Policy Statement* BEC, 1976
[13]   BTEC *BTEC Qualifications and Certificates of Achievement: the Framework* Circular 15, February 1985, p5

CURRICULAR ITEM 9
Management training through modules at Thorn EMI

Cause Structure

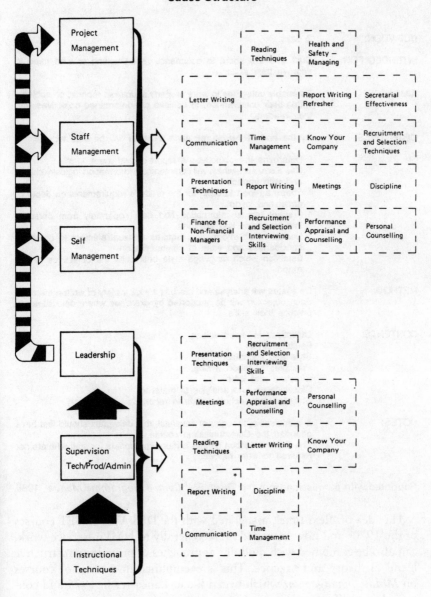

CURRICULAR ITEM 9 (continued)

REPORT WRITING

DURATION: 2 days.

INTENDED FOR: Staff who are about to commence report writing or who need to improve their skills.

AIM: To enable delegates to write properly structured reports, on subjects within their competence, to achieve pre-determined objectives with their readers.

OBJECTIVES: By the end of the course each delegate will be able to:

* Determine the objectives a report should meet.
* Use a structure which will communicate information logically, clearly and with impact.
* Shape a report to cater for the reader's requirements on depth of detail and layout.
* Present factual information and data separately from personal interpretations and opinions.
* Decide which information requires a visual element to establish conciseness and ease of communication.
* Establish which language style best suits the objectives of the report.

METHOD: Delegates will analyse and discuss a wide variety of written material. Each objective will be supported by exercises where delegates will practice their skills.

CONTENTS: Objectives in report writing.
Faults analysis.
Style and vocabulary.
Principles of report writing.
Structure and logic.
Classification and analysis of material.
Statistics and technical data in reports.

NOTES: It is advisable, though not essential, that delegates should first have attended the Communication course.
The Communication course is more appropriate for staff who are not required to write reports.

Reprinted with permission from the Thorn EMI *Course Programme Manual*, 1986

The idea of 'flexi-time', associated with the DES/ATO INSET courses of the 1970s and now extended more generally to HMI in-service work, can also be combined with modular approaches to provide an instructive blend of theory and practice. This is exemplified in a series of courses on *Middle management* which began life at Lancaster in 1975 and continued to run for some ten years.

We began with a residential weekend in which the general theory of management was explored and related to the whole school in a practical sort of way. Teachers were then asked to return to their schools and observe what was happening within them in the light of this overview. When they returned some weeks later for four days in residence at the University, this became the starting-point for a practical examination of issues which had arisen, making much use of Harold's incisive case-study technique. Next, course members returned to their schools invited to put into tentative operation some of the skills they had learnt or observed. Finally, they came back for two weekends about five weeks apart based on the topics of *The Management of Change* and *Staff Assessment.*[14]

Modules are already used for staff training within industry, as illustrated by Curricular Item 9.

For further reading

The whole problem of options is surveyed by HMI in *Aspects of Secondary Educaton* (HMSO, 1979), another useful book being M Holt's *Curriculum Workshop* (Routledge and Kegan Paul, 1983). The revision of A-level syllabuses is suggested in *AS Levels* (DES, 1984) and common core material in eleven subjects is outlined in *Common Cores at A Level* (GCE Boards, 1983). See also *Better Schools* (HMSO, 1985) for all these issues.

The linking of schools with the wider communities they serve is the theme of *British Community Primary Schools, Four Case Studies* edited by J Rennie (Falmer Press, 1985), *Parents, Teachers and Schools* edited by C Cullingford (Robert Royce, 1985), and *Communities and their Schools* edited by D Davies (McGraw Hill, 1981). First-hand accounts of individual schools are supplied by J Watts in *Towards an Open School* (Longman, 1980), by J Sharp in *Open School* (Dent, 1973) and by J Sayer in *What Future for Secondary Schools?* (Falmer Press, 1985).

Ways of liberating education from the traditional shackles of schooling are suggested in *The Free School* by W F Richmond (Methuen, 1973), *Recurrent Education* edited by V Houghton and F Richardson (Ward Lock, 1974) and *Education for the Adult Unemployed* by A H Charnley, V K McGivney and D J Sims (National Institute for Adult Continuing Education, 1986).

I Jamieson edits a series of papers on *Industry in Education* (Longman, 1985) and two more specialised books are J Eggleston's *Work Experience in Secondary Schools* (Routledge and Kegan Paul, 1982) and *Work Experience in the School Curriculum* by S Holmes, I Jamieson and J Percy (Trident Trust, 1983). An excellent collection of short case-studies is presented by the Secondary Heads' Association in *Schools and Industry* (1986).

---

[14] Warwick, D 'Middle Management in Schools' in *The Head* Vol 1, No 7, 1982, p 7

The idea of a school taking responsibility for its own in-service education is dealt with in *School-Based In-Service Education* by D Warwick (Oliver and Boyd, 1975), *Making School INSET Work* by P Easens (Croom Helm, 1985), *In School Evaluation* by M Shipman (Heinemann, 1979) and R W Morant's *In-Service Education Within the School* (Allen and Unwin, 1981). The Industrial Society's *Management in Schools* series (*Running Effective Meetings, Staff Appraisal, Decision Making* etc) could form a good basis for modular staff development as explored in this chapter. The role that may be played by parents within schools is discussed by N Beattie in *Professional Parents* (Falmer, 1985). Modular approaches in vocational work are touched upon by T A Edwards in *The Youth Training Scheme: A New Curriculum* (Falmer, 1984).

5 Modular maps

The amount of choice afforded to individuals within modular schemes varies considerably. This will depend upon a combination of factors (outlined in previous chapters) including age of pupils, nature of subject, aims of course, curricular tradition of the school, disposition of the teaching staff, external syllabuses, etc.

Very few schemes allow total freedom in this respect; while not swinging completely to the opposite (ie content - orientated) polarity of the transverse, most schools exercise a controlling influence in one of the three ways listed on page 26. These related to the tutorial function, records of progress and the pre-structuring of modules.

This chapter considers how a balance between freedom of individual choice and the need for curricular coherence may be achieved through the last of these approaches; how different pathways may be traced through the curricular material; and how alternative forms of modular mapping may be devised to meet the requirements of different schemes.

Acceptable terminology

Like most curricular innovation, modular planning is developing a terminology of its own. Anyone working in this area should be aware of it, especially if they intend entering their students for external examinations. Here, individual units are generally regarded as relating one to the other in three different kinds of way:

(a) *Complementary:* in which the modules are usually general or foundation in nature, may be taken at any time (even concurrently); performance in one is unrelated to performance in another.

(b) *Sequential:* in which a set of modules may be taken in any order but, because of their content or skill relationship, the outcome of one cannot be independent of the outcome of another.

(c) *Articulated:* in which the modules form a hierarchy and must be sequenced in time (so that completion of a first module is pre-requisite for study of the second).[1]

---

[1]   Southern Examining Group *The Modular Curriculum, a Discussion Document* 1986, p 2

This categorisation is perfectly satisfactory from an administrative point of view, but insufficiently precise for those involved in curriculum development. It is not enough merely to know that modules *articulate* – the exact nature of their relationship is important, both to those planning a course and those who may be invited to make a selection from its subsidiary units. If *sequencing* is involved, much depends on the nature of the modular chain, the purpose behind its inception, the direction in which it is heading and the extent of linkage necessary between each unit. The term *complementary* is a good one, but it has rather a different meaning in the context of modular preparation and course planning. In this case, the title derives from the interrelationship of the separate modules which together make up a single programme. From the course development point of view, modules only become 'complementary' when there is some rationality behind their selection, when some thread binds them together and gives them coherence. To state, as one group does, that units on *The History of India* and *Keyboard skills* are 'complementary' simply because they appear on the same list of units, might make administrative sense but, from the teacher's point of view, it rather suggests that modular planning is a contradiction in terms!

Answers to curricular questions such as these may be formulated if a somewhat broader division of the modular map is undertaken. Five categories are suggested: *complementary; sequential; concentric; concurrent; stratified* – and even these need some amplification through sub-divisions.

Complementary modules

If the course being followed is a particularly open and flexible one, such as is to be found at the extreme right-hand side of the transverse, there will be few restrictions over the choice of modules within it. They need not be followed in any particular order and some schemes do not even specify the age or background of pupils making the selection. Hargreaves, for example, suggests:

> If the fourth and fifth years are mixed, it might be possible for teachers to offer a wider curriculum content than at present and so allow pupils to exercise choice according to their own interests, needs and aspirations . . . By selecting an appropriate combination of units, the most able pupils can follow an accelerated course and be entered for public examinations at the end of the fourth year.[2]

Most correspondence and Open Tech courses go even further and permit almost complete freedom of access.

---

[2]   Hargreaves, D. *Improving Secondary Schools*, ILEA, 1984 para 3.11.14

Within a school or college, tutorial guidance often replaces modular pre-structuring as a basis for control, and the very flexibility of such an approach means that careful record-keeping will be necessary. The only direct stipulation is that there shall be some logical connection between the modules within any given programme, so that each adds to the individual curriculum being built up. Hence the use of the term *complementary* (see Curricular Item 10).

CURRICULAR ITEM 10
Complementary Modules,
Middleton Park High School, Leeds

Free-standing modules within a Humanities Scheme

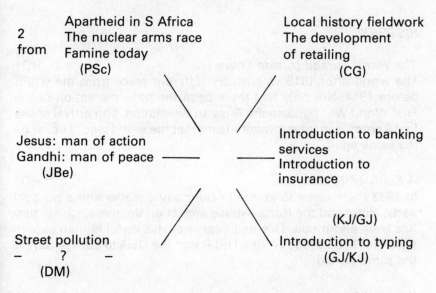

2
from

Apartheid in S Africa
The nuclear arms race
Famine today
(PSc)

Local history fieldwork
The development
of retailing
(CG)

Jesus: man of action
Gandhi: man of peace
(JBe)

Introduction to banking
services
Introduction to
insurance
(KJ/GJ)

Street pollution
– ? –
(DM)

Introduction to typing
(GJ/KJ)

Reproduced with permission from Middleton Park High School, Leeds

Any department or faculty approaching its work in this way must be absolutely certain as to the basic principles underlying the scheme and the key themes or central concepts running through it. Each and every module will then have to exemplify these features in some way – to become, as it were, a microcosm of the whole (as was seen in *The Time, Place and Society Project* outlined on page 43).

If, however, modular schemes span large areas of the curriculum, as with the Core (p.41), or general studies at Sixth Form level (p.62) as well as in more open approaches involving modular choice, then it is the specific rationale of each unit that is important and this must be spelt out in clear terms.

Sequential schemes

Slightly more structuring of individual programmes is introduced when a series of prior *sequences* is laid down. This may be done for a variety of reasons, the most obvious of which is straightforward chronology (see Curricular Item 11).

CURRICULAR ITEM 11
A Chronological Sequence, Peers School, Oxford

HISTORY

CODE

The World Turned Upside Down   HO1
The world after 1918 was a very different place from the world before 1914. Not only had there been the huge disruption of the First World War but also the Russian Revolution. The arrival of the first Communist government meant that the world would never be the same again.

A Study of Tyranny   HO2
In 1933 there came to power in Germany a leader and a political party, Hitler and the Nazis, whose impact on the twentieth century has been enormous. This unit examines this awful human experience and the attitudes of the USSR and the USA to Europe during the same period.

War and Peace   HO3
In 1939 Britain and Germany went to war. The centrepiece of this unit is a study of life in Britain during the war. Like the First World War, the Second World War made a huge impact on history. Europe declined and two superpowers, the USA and the USSR have emerged. Their rivalry has been a dominant theme since 1945. The origins of it are also included for study in this unit.

Eyeball to Eyeball   HO4
Relations between the superpowers have sometimes been called "The Cold War", describing a state of conflict which falls short of

direct confrontation on the battlefield. This unit looks at the crises as well as the periods between them and makes a study of the arms race and attempts to control it.

America in the Modern World   HO5
America has had her own problems since 1945. The most notable have been the tension brought about by the struggle of American blacks for equal civil and political rights and the effect of defeat in the long war in Vietnam.

The Wind of Change   HO6
In 1914 European powers, especially Britain, ruled over huge areas of the world, particularly in Africa and Asia. Today, with some exceptions, the peoples of the world have won independence and govern themselves. Yet there is a huge gap between the richer "North" and the poor "South", a gap which some say is more likely to lead to conflict than the differences between East and West.

Reproduced with permission from Peers School, Oxford

In this example, although the units form part of a larger chronology, they are free-standing. They are complete in themselves and each may be added to other modules from different parts of the curriculum to form different patterns. *The world turned upsidedown*, for instance, could be added to a sequence on political education; *America and the modern world* to programmes on contemporary literature or music; *Wind of change* to Geography modules dealing with different regions of the world, and so on.

Nor does a sequence of this kind necessarily have to be composed of modules from within one department alone. Two or more disciplines may combine to offer a more varied treatment, presented by several members of staff. To take another chronological example, History teachers may begin a scheme with a module relating to *the Anglo Saxons*, out of which could emerge a second on *The coming of Christianity* which, naturally, would fall to RE. This might terminate with *Norman and Angevin church building* in villages throughout the country, at which point a second unit from the History Department would supply information on *Mediaeval life*. Here Geography could take up the story, looking at *Land utilisation, past and present*. *The church in the local area* (RE) could follow, and the whole sequence be concluded by the Geography Department with *sample studies* on *Land utilisation* and a treatment of *Urbanisation*. Figure 5.1 shows this sequence in diagram form.

Figure 5.1   *An Interdisciplinary Sequence*

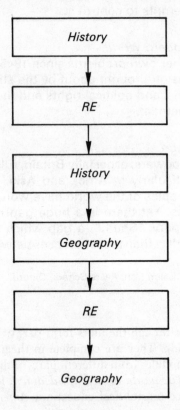

Thematic approaches

Although effective, the above is a fairly crude approach to the combination of subjects. As each retains its individual identity, it may be classified as 'interdisciplinary'. Far more subtle blending of departments (a second reason for adopting the approach in the first place), may be achieved by 'integrating' the subjects more closely or dissolving them completely into larger 'themes' (see p 14).

The Science, Geography, History and Religious Education Departments may, for example, wish to correlate aspects of their work in the middle or lower secondary age-range, taking as a general theme *The World Around Us*. Each department takes responsibility for a five-week module (see Figure 5.2). This individual module may either be unilateral or fully

Figure 5.2   *The Thematic Approach*

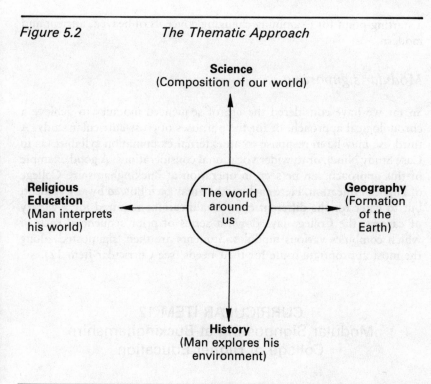

integrated, involving a cross-disciplinary team in its planning and teaching. In the latter case, however, one Department takes a leading role in each unit, according to its content.

An interesting way of dealing with this could be to link the content even further by relating it to *The four elements*. Under the title *Composition of our world*, the Science Department might deal with the life-giving properties of the atmosphere and earth, using water and fire to represent potential and kinetic energy respectively. Geography could take on responsibility for *Formation of the Earth*, including land-formation (earth), climate (air), and the effects of water and fire (glaciation, volcanoes, earthquakes, etc). Historians, thinking about *People explore the environment*, would almost certainly wish to include exploration by land, sea and air, and could cover 'fire' by looking at inventions such as gunpowder, steam locomotion, rocketry, etc. Religious Education's part in the scheme would be of a more symbolic nature, and provide a commentary upon the whole. The mythology of the Old Testament and Christ's teaching in the New are shot through with the imagery of fire and water, which has in turn been incorporated into the sacraments and liturgy of the church. Earth suggests some treatment of the creation, and Air perhaps a starting-point for examining changing concepts of heaven, ancient and modern.

Modular signposting

So far we have considered the use of sequenced modules to achieve a chronological approach, or for the purposes of cross-curricular study. A third use may be in response to an external examination syllabus (as in Case Study Nine), or to wider vocational considerations. A good example of this approach can be seen in operation at Buckinghamshire College of Higher Education. Here each module may be followed by any student, but to cater for the different entry qualifications required for a variety of careers, the College lays down a series of prior sequences, each of which combines various modules. Students are then 'signposted' along the most appropriate route for their needs (see Curricular Item 12).

CURRICULAR ITEM 12
Modular Signposting at Buckinghamshire College of Higher Education

Course Streams

The set of option modules has been designed to allow students a flexible and coherent pattern of choice within three broad streams, chosen to reflect established career opportunities.

Accountancy Stream
Marketing Stream
Personnel Stream

Each course stream comprises a 'package' of four option modules, two taken during each stage, which allows students to select a coherent package possibly related to their intended career, while still reflecting their broader interests in the two remaining option modules. The recommended groupings for the four streams are as follows:

Accountancy: Accounting Practice, Business Law, Business Data Systems, Quantitative Business Analysis/Business Economics.

Marketing   Marketing Principles, Business Law, Market Research and Planning, International Marketing/ Marketing Sales and Communications.

Personnel   Personnel Studies, Business Law, Personnel Resource Management, Industrial Relations.

The remaining two option modules can be chosen freely during each stage of the course, and could comprise, for example, Modern Language I and II.

The course streams have been designed particularly to answer the requirements of certain professional institutions in terms of offering exemptions from various stages of their professional examinations.

Reproduced with permission from the *School of Management Studies and Languages Prospectus* Buckingham College of Higher Education, p 8.

The concentric model

The use of a *concentric* model, in which key modules provide the essential core of a discipline or course, was described in Chapter 2 (page 26). Here, each optional module extends and develops the work of the core and, through differing combinations of optional units, varied degrees of specialisation may be achieved. A good example is the Northern Partnership for Records of Achievement's Modular Science Course at GCSE level. The central core here is:

- materials and their use
- man – a living organism
- the environment
- energy

These combine with optional modules (see Curricular Item 13) to give certificates relating either to General Science or more specifically geared to Physics, Biology, etc.

A set of key modules containing such material may be introduced at the beginning of a course and followed by optional units that relate back to them (rather as the phenomenological approach to Comparative Religion was treated on page 20). Alternatively, core modules may run alongside all other units throughout the course. Again, core units may appear at the end of a course. Curricular Item 14 shows the double module with which the Cambridgeshire TVEI Consortium insist all students complete their 'A' level Art and Design Course.

CURRICULAR ITEM 13
Optional UNITS in NEA's Modular Science Scheme

Option Module Title	Bio-logical	Physical	Environ-mental	Rural	Techno-logical
Physical Behaviour Patterns		*			
Making Useful New Stuff		*			
Colour	*	*			
Information and Communication					*
Geological Science			*		
It's Very Disturbing			*		
Water, Water Everywhere			*		
Electronics					*
Flight					*
Radioactivity		*			
(Under Development)					
Sound, Light and Such Things		*			
Metals		*			
Living Things: Design	*				
Living Things: Variety	*				
Food for Thought	*		*		
Structures					*
Mechanisms					*
Science of Motor Vehicles		*			
Sports Science	*				
Biotechnology	*				
Getting the best out of plants:					
1 Protected cultivation				*	
2 Outdoor cultivation				*	
3 Arable cultivation/forestry			*	*	
Getting the best out of animals			*	*	

CURRICULAR ITEM 14
Compulsory Core Module, Cambridgeshire Consortium
A Level TVEI

MODULE TITLE   *STUDENT PROJECT*   *Ref No ADSP 2*

STUDENT GUIDANCE SHEET

This double module is intended to provide you with a real opportunity to develop the skills and ideas you have accrued through your four modular courses. It is not the intention of the syllabus to prescribe themes or design briefs for you but rather to challenge you to develop your own aims and objectives based on the experience you have gained. You might wish to pursue work that you began in a previous module or perhaps a suitable theme for development has evolved from your working notebook/sketchbook. Whatever you decide should be done in consultation with your teacher/s.

You will need to identify one or at most two areas of study. For instance you might be developing a painting topic but this would not preclude drawing skills or photography if you find them appropriate to certain aspects of your work.

You could choose a thematic topic, eg shells, building etc which you would like to develop. Different media could be used here because the coherence would be provided by the theme.

Assessment will be based on the same criteria as the modules but will include marking of your response to your own chosen theme or project.*

Reproduced with permission from *Modular A Levels in Art and Design* Cambridge-shire TVEI Consortium, 1986, p 25

*NB *This module should not be confused with the 'Common cores' at Advanced Level prepared by the GCE Boards of England, Wales and Northern Ireland* (see page 55)

It could be decided, of course, that as long as these key modules are taken at some point, it does not really matter when they are tackled. The 'core' may be reached at various junctures in each individual's programme of work, providing a different perspective according to whether it is dealt with near the beginning, middle or end. However, to leave the selection of core modules so much to chance could lead, in some cases, to unbalanced courses where core units follow one another in quick succession. Many schools therefore either 'cycle' students round key modules on a termly or half-yearly basis, or institute regular joint presentations or 'lead lessons'. These are given by the Head of Department or teams of teachers and serve to link up all optional modules in progress (see Figure 5.3).

Figure 5.3

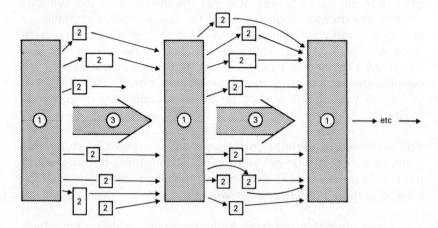

1 Lead lesson
2 Optional modules (3–6 weeks)
3 Planning and preparation by course team

The concurrent approach

The approaches so far described began at the far right-hand of the modular transverse and through them we have moved progressively further along it. The pre-structuring of material has increased with each step – complementary modules, sequences which incorporate fully integrated themes, interdisciplinary work, units of related studies and the use of curricular signposting. With each step, the control a school has over the choice of modules increases.

With the *Concentric* and *Concurrent* approaches we reach a halfway point on the transverse. Here, some freedom of choice may be available, but it is likely to be circumscribed.

Within *concurrent* patterns two or more related modules operate alongside one another. It is important that the same students attend them, so choice tends to be restricted. So, for example, the Art Department may wish to run a module on *Impressionist Art* and arrange for this to be strengthened by one from the Music Department along the same lines; the Maths Department may be asked by Geography to assist in their work on *rainfall and temperature* by offering a short module on *graphs*. In cases such as these, each module would be independent yet run along parallel lines, having continual cross-references and links with the other. But much may be gained from an even closer liason. To facilitate this, the following types of sequence might be arranged (Fig 5.4).

Figure 5.4

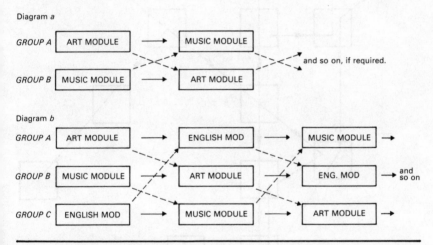

Diagram *a*

GROUP A | ART MODULE → MUSIC MODULE

GROUP B | MUSIC MODULE → ART MODULE

and so on, if required.

Diagram *b*

GROUP A | ART MODULE → ENGLISH MOD → MUSIC MODULE →

GROUP B | MUSIC MODULE → ART MODULE → ENG. MOD → and so on

GROUP C | ENGLISH MOD → MUSIC MODULE → ART MODULE →

Stratification

The least flexible of all modular programmes are those which pre-specify the precise order in which the different component units will be followed and restrict their use to those taking certain courses. When this stage has been reached, we are at the extreme left-hand side of the transverse.

In a purely *stratified* programme, Stage One must be mastered before Stage Two can be tackled; Stage Two is essential for the understanding of Stage Three, and so on. Failure to come to terms with any of these stages within the sequence will result in the breakdown of the whole process for the person concerned. He will be able to take his study only as far as this point; beyond that, all is suspect.

Modular stratification can be represented in diagram form as follows:

Figure 5.5

Modular sequencing

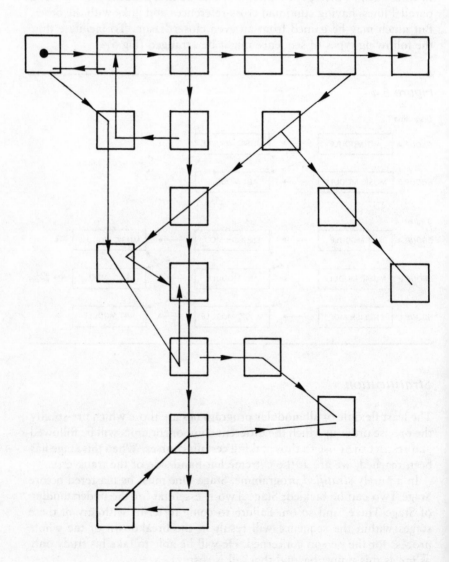

Stratification and Sequencing Compared

Stratified modules

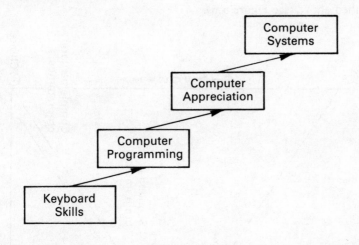

Diversified schemes

A modular scheme does not, of course, have to confine itself to a single approach. The TVEI 'taster units' (illustrated on page 13) introduced the idea of students experiencing a range of approaches before deciding upon the direction in which they wished to continue. Under CPVE regulations Introductory Modules (see page 31) may be followed either concurrently or consecutively.

The concentric approach, by placing its key modules at strategic points during the year, can convert the 'levels' associated with stratified planning into a series of 'plateaux', from which limited choice may be available.

One of the strengths of such schemes is the possibility they open up for students to change direction at a later stage than is normally possible. This allows those who reach their academic peak in the middle of a stratified scheme to transfer to programmes of a more complementary or sequential nature. Concurrent modules may also be adapted to suit any of the approaches outlined in this chapter.

Modules in fully open schemes should be considered multi-dimensional – in other words, they may be utilised in very different ways by different students, possibly as part of separate courses.

Modifying the transverse

The model for modular planning, introduced on page 18 and outlined in Chapter Two, can now be modified to accommodate the approaches described above (see Figure 5.6).

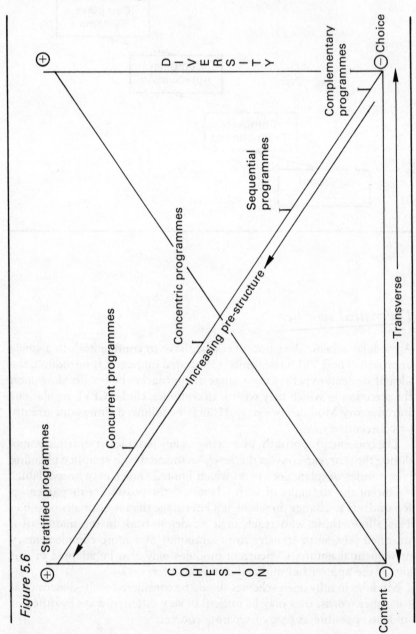

Figure 5.6

For further reading

The epistemological ideas covered in this chapter may be followed up in a number of books, including: *Crisis in the Curriculum* edited by E C Cuff and G C F Payne (Croom Helm, 1985), *Practical Curriculum Study* by P Barnes (Routledge and Kegan Paul, 1982) *Curriculum Structure and Design* by D Warwick (Hodder and Stoughton, 1975), *Thinking about the Curriculum* by W A Reid (Routledge and Kegan Paul, 1978), *Disciplines of the Curriculum*, edited by R C Whitfield, (RKP, 1972), *The Challenge of Curriculum Change* by T Dalton (Falmer, 1987) and the various *GCSE Guidelines* issued by the Secondary Examination Council (SEC). M Marland and S Hills stress the importance of good management at this level in *Departmental Management* (Heinemann, 1981) while D John widens the field in *Leadership in Schools* (Heinemann, 1980). In this context, see also *Developing Management in Schools* by K B Everard (Basil Blackwell, 1986).

6 Preparation and Planning

The module, or single unit of work, is the basic element of all the schemes described in this book. It is the building block from which each individual programme is constructed or, alternatively, it forms a single constituent part in a larger course of study. Its flexibility can therefore make a major contribution to the curriculum. Another is its power to motivate pupils through short-term goals or objectives spelt out in terms of what is 'known, understood and to be done'.[1] This, in turn, encourages a lively two-way exchange of ideas between teacher and taught.

Timetabling

There is no 'golden rule' about the length of a module, nor the number of hours that should be spent on it. Six to eight weeks is the usual time-span, as this fits neatly into the duration of the school year, allowing two modules per term and additional time for administrative and assessment procedures. With young children the 'targets' may need to be set closer together, so that the intermediary goals do not seem so far ahead; with older students modules could be stretched to last a whole term.

Another consideration is an epistemological one. As the Southern Examining Group points out:

> Modular structures can compromise many very small modules or a few very large ones. The drive for short term curriculum goals suggests that they should be small but the guiding principle should be that they should be educationally satisfying and coherent in their own right. Experience shows that modules designed for 20–30 hours of study are able to satisfy these criteria, and at the same time, permit a desirable balance between 'formative' and 'summative' assessment.[2]

There is, of course, no reason why every module should be of the same length. Within one course a certain piece of work may require a short, fairly vivid presentation: others may necessitate lengthier, more detailed

---

[1] GCSE *General Criteria* para 16.
[2] Southern Examining Group *The Modular Curriculum: A Discussion Document* 1986, p2

study. Timetabling becomes difficult under these circumstances, as it does if considerable flexibility is required to enable individuals to take varying lengths of time to complete the same tasks, or to provide for different pupils working simultaneously on modules of differing length.

One response is to classify the units as 'Half', 'Double' or even 'Quarter' modules, lasting respectively four, sixteen or two weeks. Another is to block the timetable so that within certain areas teams of teachers have complete freedom as to how they organise their work. This could mean a return to the worst excesses of the faculty system, but it does have the great merit of enabling group size, length of module, contribution of staff, style of teaching, allocation of resources and duration of lesson all to conform to the requirements of the curriculum being developed, rather than vice-versa.

Planning the work

No matter how free-standing they may be, modules are not ends in themselves, but part of a larger organisation, be this a school, college, university or industrial concern. As such, they are subsumed within the larger educational process to which the parent–body is committed. The aims, objectives and methodology of each should therefore be completely in line with this set of more comprehensive, all-embracing goals. These goals should, in turn, be enshrined in the work of each subsidiary division of the school – its departments, faculties, houses or years – and it is at this level that most modular work will take place.

As part of the process of meeting institutional goals, and in order to achieve curricular coherence, all members of the team entrusted with a modular scheme need to be fully involved in its outline planning at the very least. How much greater their involvement with the scheme as a whole may be depends largely upon the nature of the course and various external constraints.

The course may consist of a series of very tightly-linked modules – it may be highly stratified, or linked vertically through a number of concurrent units. Obviously, these must be considered in relation to each other if fragmentation or loss of direction is not to occur. This is especially important if students are to be entered for an external examination. Some Boards are now offering fully modularised programmes, which have built-in safeguards: they may specify the kind of records they wish to be kept throughout the development of the course or, in more open courses, lay down explicit submission requirements with a moderator being appointed for each school (see Curricular Item 41 and 45).

In concentric courses, in which core modules feature, these key elements should be planned by the team as a whole , or at least, by a small group following full discussion of content and treatment. This will establish the interrelationship of the work, and the modules will be seen to link more readily into a coherent programme.

Optional modules will probably be allocated to individuals or small groups to plan separately. But the rationale for the choice must be clear to all. Most frequently, it will relate to some specific contribution that the teacher can make: specialised knowledge, relevant skill, research interest, qualification or out-of-school activity. The teacher, or the group with whom he works for this purpose, will now have ownership of the unit. As a result, it is likely to be lively and carefully planned, since it has to stand up to the scrutiny of the rest of the team in a way an individual's work very rarely does under conventional curricular arrangements. Being based on a positive contribution that its planner has to make, such modules should have enthusiasm built in from the outset – and enthusiasm is a contagious commodity. From here it is but a short step to building up a curriculum around the individual enthusiasms – academic and otherwise – of all who work in a school.

Having prepared their modules, individuals or groups will need to report back to the team as a whole for their work to be ratified. The modular specification (see page 113) should be presented a week or so in advance and the planners should indicate precisely how it fits into the overall curricular map which is being prepared. In some cases, this link may need to be very explicit, as in stratified schemes, in others, the approach may be far more multi-dimensional, as in complementary programmes.

This sort of team planning should answer the major criticism made of modular schemes – that fragmentation can occur if those teaching them are not fully aware of what is going on in other parts of the course. Cross-referencing between modules may be needed, even if this simply entails calling upon students who have followed certain units to brief the current group at the appropriate time. If the teacher has no knowledge of the content, let alone the titles, of other units, there is no chance of arranging even this.

There should also be some system whereby those teachers not involved in modular planning can be kept informed about the progress of such schemes. Not only is it divisive to have an 'in group' operating within an institution, it also means that other curricular areas are deprived of the opportunity to link up with the programme, should they ever wish to do so.

Modular banking

The joint discussion of individual modules is of particular importance when schools reach the point of modular banking – that is, of having on file a series of free-standing modules which may be slotted in or out of a course at short notice in response to demand. With such a system it is likely that those responsible for presenting a unit may not have been directly involved in its preparation – but they can at least discuss its inclusion and have the opportunity to modify the format at an early stage in the proceedings.

Of course, the treatment of any module will vary according to those who teach it and those who make it part of their programme, but the more pre-structured a scheme the less opportunities there are for this to happen.

The currency of modules 'banked' in this way is usually strongest either when those who prepared them are also responsible for their presentation, or when the unit relates directly to local history, the direct environment of the school or specific resources that are available. Teachers may come and go, but the parish church, the nature conservancy, the information office or a photographic dark-room are relatively stable features in the scholastic landscape. A special feature of modular banking is the close attention that needs to be paid to the groupwork, projects, activities, etc it encompasses. The essence of such units is that they are available at short notice and this, combined with the fact that the teacher may come fresh to the topic, means that they should be as 'user friendly' as possible! A typical banked module from the pastoral curriculum is reproduced as Curricular Item 15 (see pages 104–12).

The point has already been made that units such as this require an adequate system of record-keeping if they are to be of use to teachers, tutors and students. A record-card such as that shown in Figure 6.1 carefully filed and kept up to date, is very necessary.

Figure 6.1

TITLE .... CODE ....

LEVEL .... PREPARED BY ....

LENGTH .... GROUP SIZE ....

MATERIALS PROVIDED ....

....

RESOURCES REQUIRED ....

SUGGESTED APPROACH ....

DATE PREPARED ....

UP-DATED & COMMENTS ....

....

CURRICULAR ITEM 15
Banked Module from Pastoral Curriculum,
Farnham College, Surrey.

AGONY AUNT

Aim

This pack contains letters supposedly written to Aunt Maud, who dispenses weekly doses of good advice from a national magazine. Use the letters in any way you wish to generate discussion in the group, to evince sympathy with the writers, to share common problems or to place the students in other peoples' shoes.

Organisation

It is suggested that only one or two of the letters are considered at a time and there would seem to be three main ways of doing this:

a   The whole group reads and discusses the letter(s). In this way every member of the group shares the problem and can contribute to every stage of the debate.

b   In sub-groups of about four students, discuss the same letter or letters. Each sub-group then reports back on their preferred solution briefly, then there can be general discussion of the solutions advanced. In this way each individual discusses a single issue in a small group and general discussion concentrates on three or four possible solutions. This is a good way of showing that a single problem can generate several different, equally acceptable solutions.

c   In sub-groups as above, discuss different letters. The group as a whole then reads all the letters under consideration and hears the suggested solutions. Discussion will be somewhat curtailed with this approach, but each individual will have had a say on some issue. With this approach a range of problems are tackled in a less deep or penetrating manner.

Approach

You know your group better than anyone, so you are the best person to decide on the kind of approach that would be most fruitful. However, I do suggest that you:

–   Use only one or two letters at a time, either in plenary of sub-group discussion.

- Avoid too great a 'build up' to the exercise; invariably this puts students very much on their guard.

- At all cost avoid easy, flip answers given without too much thought.

- Neither reject minority views nor acccept wholeheartedly majority ones. There are no 'right solutions' to these problems; it is a completely 'open' exercise.

- Act as a 'neutral chairperson' but do not be afraid of asking the question that no one else has or getting individuals to elaborate on what they have said.

Follow up

'Agony Aunt' is complete in itself and there is no need whatsoever to follow it up if you do not wish to. Here, though, are some ways in which you could develop the work:

1   Take some further letters from the pack and do the exercise in a different way (see 'Organisation' above).

2   Write an answer to one of the letters as Aunt Maud might have penned it.

3   If you think one or more of the letters puts the ideas across in a poor or slovenly fashion, re-write in such a way to gain sympathy from Aunt Maud.

4   Role play one or more of the solutions advanced by the group.

5   Write other letters to Aunt Maud to be discussed at a later session by the group.

6   Write letters from your group to another tutor group, to which they have to give a written reply.

7   Send one of the letters to two or more Agony Aunts working for magazines and see what happens!

8   Organise an 'Open Forum' consisting of staff and students from your Senior Tutor Group and see what they say about some of these letters.

TRG/KY3/9/WW/1.4.85

Canterbury
Kent.

Dear Auntie Maud,

I read your column each week and find it most interesting. Your advice is always useful and you have no idea how much help it is to your readers.

Now, my own problem. My boyfriend who I have been going out with, for about two years, has arranged for a group of us, girls and boys, to go off together on a camping holiday in Devon. When my Mum and Dad heard about this they almost had kittens! My Dad seems to think we will spend the entire time leaping in and out of bed with one another. Mum, well all she seems worried about is what the neighbours and the relatives will think!

Honestly, anyone would think that I was ten, not seventeen! Do they think I can't look after myself, or am immoral? And, anyway, what business is it of their's how I spend my holiday?

Yours sincerely

Ann Keating

TRG/KY3/8/WW/1.4.85

Foxgloves
Raymond Avenue
Bournemouth

Dear Auntie Maud,

What shall I do? I find life at college so tedious and the thought of three more years at University appalls me. They say I am clever. I suppose I am, (three grade D's and two B's at O'levels) but what I <u>really</u> want to do is serve in the shop where I work each weekend and some evenings.

I am also supposed to be good with the customers and do so enjoy the relaxed, informal atmosphere, dealing with problems as they arise and selling things. Now I have been offered several jobs in the locality and would love to accept each and every-one of them. However, my parents will not hear of this. They really have set their minds on having a daughter at University. My teachers say I ought to get in as well.

Must I really go on to higher education just to please others?

Love

Fiona Spender.

TRG/KY3/7/WW/1.4.85

4 Willow Close
Lindhurst
BP04 8X

Dear Maud,

I don't read your column but my girlfriend does, and she's persuaded me to write. Here's a <u>real</u> problem for you!

For the last three months I have been applying for jobs and been told by my parents, friends, girlfriend, teachers, relatives, well-wishers and other multifarious members of the 'establishment' that I must present the 'right' (in <u>BOTH</u> senses of the word!) image.

Regardless of my three A levels and seven O levels, this - apparently - consists of: wearing a suit, white shirt, tie, polishing my shoes eh, eh, eh mm and answering politely when I am spoken to, definitely <u>NOT</u> asking questions, and speaking with a correct Oxbridge accent.

All this I regard as C--P! If they want to see the <u>real</u> me, then why should I pretend to be what I am <u>NOT</u>?? I <u>hate</u> suits and refuse not to say what I think. To do otherwise would be bourgeoise hypocrisy - the kind of attitude ~~that~~

cont.

that has got this country
where it is now — in the gutter!!

So, now what do you think??
And please, don't lets have any
of your boring, meaningless platitudes. My g/friend may lap
them up, but I don't!!

Ken Rivers

TRG/KY3/6/WW/1.4.85

> 53 Makepiece Street,
> Bolton,
> Lancashire,
> BU16 9TL.

Dear Aunt Maud,

      Please do help me. I am in a very diificult situation and I don't know what to do. Also, excuse the typing, I am doing this on Dad's typewriter whilst he is out!

    A few months ago I agreed to go out with a boy who lives on our estate. He is quite pleasant and well-meaning but, go be honest, I do find him rather uninteresting. We have now been out together several times and now I just can't seem to get rid of him. He rings up about twice a week and, although I make various excuses, he just doesn't get the message. HE hangs roundthe house and always seems to be popping up wheN I%am out with 'friends? On Valentine'sDay he sent me an embarrassing ly affectionate card and now he has just sent a most exrpnsave present for my birthday, quite spoiling the dAy for me.'

    The trouble is, he is so sensitive that I just dare not tell him outright how I feel. ALso I ought to return thecpresent, but he will be so upset. Now I feel like a prisoner, I can't go out with other boys for fear of upsetting him, yet don't want to go on seeing this one.

    HoW can I best let him know the way things are?

                Yours anxiously;

                Janet

                (MISS J. RyDER)

TRG/KY3/5/Ww/1.4.85

21 Dewhurst Road,

Poole,

Dorset.

Dear Aunt Maud,

My girlfriend, who I love dearly, has just taken up smoking. In fact she now stinks like a factory chimney. The very thought of kissing her is repulsive to a non-smoker.

She says that I am childish and immature. Perhaps I am, — but must I really choose between her and tobacco? Or do you think, like Mary (my girlfriend) does, that I will get used to it in time?

Yours Sinerely

James Goodal.

TRG/KY3/4/Ww/1.4.85

14 Worcester Lane
Didcot,
Berkshire

Dear Aunt Maud,
    What does one do with a
sarcastic teacher who keeps
picking on one?
    My friends tell me that I
should complain to the headmaster,
but I really don't want to get
the man into trouble. After all
he does seem to get on well
with everyone else. I feel
that if I consult my parents
they will take some action
that will really embarrass.
Believe me, I have dropped
enough hints that I don't like
that tone of voice, and I can't
very well tell him, can I.
    What do you advise?

            Yours Sincerly
            Janine Miller

TRG/KY3/3/Ww/1.4.85   2 SPAR ROAD,
                            SCARBOROUGH,
                            N. YORKSHIRE,
                            GL16 9CV

Dear A. M..
            My grandad has just died and
mum seems awfully upset about it.
There are now just the two of us and I
feel that I ought to be able to comfort her
somehow. But I am no good with words.
What shall I do?
                        Yours truly,
                        Graham Anderson

Modular specification

It is difficult to be precise about the exact manner in which a module is
prepared. Every subject in the curriculum, or any combination of subjects,
may be tackled in this way, and the approach can be adopted at all levels
from primary through to university, and used with students of all ages
– from infants to members of adult education classes. What is more, the
modular approach is ideal for community schools, or colleges in which
the curriculum operates for all those who enrol – children, parents and/or
grandparents included (see p.65)!

A useful model to have in mind from the outset is an industrial one
which relates to the specification of a job, implement, artifact, contract,
etc, in fairly general terms. The model takes the whole process of design
and development through a number of stages, ensuring that the finished
product actually measures up to what it is intended to do, that it is
adequately resourced and that modifications may be made as and when
they are required.

The relevance of such an approach to this area of the curriculum can
be seen in the nature of modules themselves. Some have to fit precisely
into pre-planned programmes, some are selected by individual students
as part of an à la carte menu of options, while others may be 'banked'
for future use. In each case, the exact nature of the unit has to be clear

and, what is more, it has to 'deliver the goods', in other words, perform the functions claimed by its authors. There has to be a means of assessing whether it does this or not and, in the case of modules which fail to measure up, it is vital to have a system whereby modifications may be effected.

CURRICULAR ITEM 16
An industrial model for specification

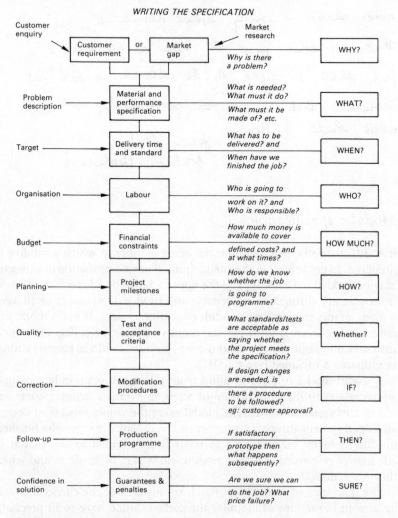

Reproduced by permission of M. Dobson

The industrial specification shown in Curricular Item 16 is fairly easy to follow and can readily be translated into curricular terms.

Modules may arise either to fill an identified *gap in the market* – some part of an articulated course which is not adequately covered or has received inadequate treatment, or through *customer enquiry* – student demand.

Performance specification here entails just what the module is intended to do, and how it does it. The central *aim* of the module must be made clear, and broken down into *objectives*. These state categorically what the pupils will be doing – but not necessarily how they will approach the task. Eisner, in particular, has developed the idea of 'expressive outcomes' in which 'it is legitimate for the end result to surprise the teacher and the student'.[3]

Both aims and objectives may be considered in terms of:

- *Concepts*: the key ideas, basic themes or mental patterns contained within the module.
- *Skills*: mental or physical competencies learnt through practice.
- *Behaviours*: personal and inter-personal actions, traits or dispositions that need to be encouraged.

Objectives are always couched positively, by the use of strong, transitive verbs. Consider, for example, just a few of the activities that are part of the core material in *A Basis for Choice*.[4] Students are here invited to:

interview	distinguish
visit	listen to
make comparisons	explain
identify	make notes on
participate in	appreciate
present	question
compare	choose
obtain information about	check
recognise	indicate
experience	plan
develop awareness of	read
perform	demonstrate knowledge of
practice	formulate
observe	apply
appraise	give reasons for
encounter	adopt behaviour
analyse	consider

---

[3] Quoted in Lenten, T., Darby, M., Miller, S. and Sibbel, H. *Praxis* Secondary Art/Craft Standing Committee, Victoria, 1981, p43.

[4] See FEU *A Basis for Choice* 1979, pp.48–73.

Roger Lewis further develops the idea of planning through objectives in *How to Help Learners Assess their Progress*[5], as Curricular Item 17 shows.

CURRICULAR ITEM 17
Strong and Weak Objectives

Strong features	Weak features
Describe learner outcome eg, to list three main principles of marketing	Refer to teacher behaviour eg, to cover the main principles the teacher will lead a discussion on the main principles of marketing
Are specific eg, given a format, can produce a marketing plan for a new product	Are general eg, understand about planning and marketing for a new product
Describe observable outcomes eg, states three reasons why the small businessman must consider marketing	Describe states of mind eg, understands why marketing is important
Describe behaviour eg, list three main principles of marketing	Describe subject matter eg, the main principles of marketing
Builds on the strengths of the learners as identified at the course planning stage eg, apply the three principles to your own business	Ignore existing strengths of learners
Clear; concise eg, list three ways in which you promote a product	Ambiguous; wordy eg, explain some of the methods and strategies which a business may use in order to bring a particular and specified product to the knowledge of relevant and important sections of the public
Covers one outcome eg, 1 identify the information you require to . . . 2 locate the information	Covers several outcomes eg, identify and locate the information you require to . . .

[5]   Lewis, R. *How to Help Learners Assess their Progress*, CET, 1985.

Leads easily to an assessment item eg, the following objective recognises three reasons why the small businessman must consider marketing leads to: – the following are five reasons given for marketing. Tick the three that, according to the author, are the most important.	No clear and easy path to an assessment item eg, understands why marketing is important leads to where?

It is not easy to show 'good' and 'bad' examples of objectives in the abstract. Much depends, of course, on the nature of each scheme and in particular on the characteristics of the learners.

Reproduced with permission from: R. Lewis, *How to Help Learners Assess their Progress*, CET, 1984. pp.97–98.

Hemsworth High help their staff clarify the issue even further with cogent advice presented in a particularly engaging fashion (Curricular Item 18).

Note that the outcomes here need to be especially clear and measurable, as most units are submitted for external accreditation. Compare also the 'sub-categories' suggested with those given on page 115. The standardisation of all such records throughout the school both makes the teachers' task easier (see Chapter 10) and – if required – facilitates the construction of coherent programmes of work.

To return to the industrial specification, the *Target* is self-explanatory, and includes the date by which the module has to be presented to the rest of the team and the level at which it is pitched. Similarly, *Organisation* refers to the staff responsible for teaching the unit as well as the methodology to be employed. Here consideration might be given to the strategies drawn up by the S W Region Curriculum Base, and shown in Curricular Item 19.

Under *Budget* are included the materials, equipment, facilities and specialised rooms (science laboratory, art room, etc.) that may be required, together with a range of items outside the school.

The *Planning* section encompasses the interrelationship between groups planning modules and the team as a whole referred to earlier in this chapter, as well as the monitoring of any scheme once it has begun. It will later be suggested that a system of record-keeping is employed, not only to keep track of individuals' progress through the scheme but also as a form of quality control over the modules themselves. This will lead to correction as and when required.

Follow-up and *Confidence in solution* refer both to the individual modules themselves and to administrative details (see Chapter 7) at one level, and the scheme as a whole at another.

CURRICULAR ITEM 18
Preparing Units for Accreditation,
Hemsworth High School, Yorkshire

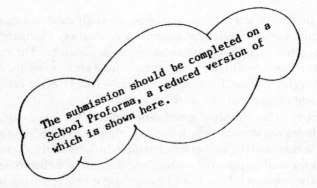

UNIT ACCREDITATION   CODE:
SUBMISSION UNIT PROFORMA   DATE:

SCHOOL: HEMSWORTH HIGH SCHOOL.   L.E.A.:   WAKEFIELD

UNIT TITLE:

CURRICULAR AREA:

UNIT DESCRIPTION:

OUTCOMES TO BE ASSESSED   EVIDENCE TO BE OFFERED

The submission should be completed on a School Proforma, a reduced version of which is shown here.

PROCEDURES FOR MAKING AND RECORDING ASSESSMENT

1

UNIT TITLE

a) Must be meaningful to the users of the Letter of Credit. Over—technical expressions should be avoided, e.g. Body Performance is better than Applied Physiology.

b) If you intend to produce more units on the same theme, consider carefully the implications of using a particular title, if it restricts consequent titles. It may be better to plan a number of titles from the beginning.

CURRICULAR AREA

This should detail the Department(s)/subject(s) involved, e.g.

'Domestic Electricity' - Physical Science
'Use of Resources' - History/Science

2

UNIT DESCRIPTION

Describe the unit briefly, in terms of
the learning objectives and processes
involved, and the educational context
in which learning will take place:

   Some examples

LEARNING OBJECTIVES, e.g. '... develop
their awareness of. ....

STYLE OF COURSE, e.g. 'The students
will follow a practically based
course ......'

HOW STUDENTS WILL LEARN,e.g. 'This will
be achieved through ...... ' or '.....
they will investigate ....by ......'

OUTCOMES TO BE ASSESSED

Outcomes must be:

a) observable during the process and/or identifiable in the product

b) clearly related to the unit title/description

c) broken down into one or more of the following sub-categories:

  1. **ABILITIES** or skills to be demonstrated

  2. **KNOWLEDGE** which the student will show

  3. **CONCEPTS** to be understood

  4. **PROCESSES** to be experienced

On the Proforma the wording of the **OUTCOMES SECTION** must be phrased as follows:

In completing this unit the student will have .....

1. Demonstrated an ability to ...

2. Shown knowledge of ...

3. Acquired an understanding of ...

4. Experienced ...

4

¦OUTCOMES¦ (continued)

N.B.   Outcomes should be numbered sequentially, ignoring
       the four different elements.   For example, A is
       correct but B and C are **not**.

A	B	C
Demonstrated an	Demonstrated an	Demonstrated an
ability to	ability to	ability to ....
1.	1.	1a.
2.	2.	1b.
3.	3.	2.
Shown knowledge	Shown knowledge	Shown knowledge
of	of	of ....
4.	1.	3.
5.	2.	4a.
6.	3.	4b.

Where a statement seems a little vague try to provide
an example to clarify what is meant,

i.e.   'Simple apparatus will be used to ......
       e.g. a stop watch'.

OR   'Measure the force used in simple actions,
       e.g. pushing or pulling.

OUTCOMES FOR GROUP WORK should be specified in the
following way:

'To participate as a member of a group in the
......' rather than merely putting, 'To produce ...'

5

EVIDENCE TO BE OFFERED

The relationship between each outcome and the evidence
to be offered must be clearly shown by means of numerical
cross-referencing,

e.g. Student compiled record containing,

    a. The results and conclusions of
        practical work   (1 to 4)

    b. Written work, in the form of
        descriptions, problems and
        questions.   (5 to 7)

    c. Diagrams with comments   (8, 9)

    Teacher's record   (1, 3, 4)

'Student compiled record (1 to 9)' is too vague a
statement.

N.B. A student will only receive accreditation if ALL
the evidence is available to show he/she has
successfully completed each and every outcome. If your
submission states that two different types of
evidence will be used to demonstrate that an outcome
has been achieved, then BOTH MUST BE PROVIDED.

Since it is only necessary to offer one form of
evidence in your submission you are strongly
advised to AVOID REPLICATION OF EVIDENCE.

6

Evidence of a students achievements can be grouped under a number of headings:

1. **PRIMARY EVIDENCE** in the form of, for example, a piece of written work or a finished product.

2. **PRIMARY EVIDENCE** in the form of, for example, a tape or video recording or a photograph.

3. **SECONDARY EVIDENCE** in the form of a record, completed by the teacher, the student or both together.

Please see definitions of "TEACHER'S/STUDENT'S RECORD and CHECKLISTS".

PROCEDURES FOR MAKING AND RECORDING ASSESSMENT

At present a general statement of the methods used is satisfactory, e.g.

The teacher's records and comments on individual student's achievements of the outcomes, in the evidence described above, will be available in the form of detailed statements showing the date that each student has satisfactorily completed each item of evidence. The student's record book will also be available.

As we move towards 'levels' within the system, we can expect this section to become increasingly detailed.

IT WILL TAKE AT LEAST SEVEN WEEKS FROM SUBMITTING A UNIT TO IT BEING APPROVED

CURRICULAR ITEM 19
Learning Strategies for CPVE

Reflective learning

Reviews: Diaries; Logs; Groupwork; Exhibitions; Brainstorming; Case Studies; Surveys; Questionnaires; Tutorials; Seminars.

Experiential learning

Role Play; Simulation and Games; Groupwork; Design; Modelling; Work Experience and Vocational Extension; Fieldwork; Surveys; Prototypes; Experiments.

Resource based learning

Projects; Design; Demonstrations; Brainstorming; Fieldwork; Team Teaching; Research; Instruction.

Reproduced by permission of S W Region Curriculum Base

Checklist

The more individuals within a team know about the nature of the modules their colleagues are developing, the easier it is for them to ensure cross-referencing both within the material they write and in the actual teaching of the course. Students' choice of modules will be facilitated, and the advice given by tutors regarding the composition of programmes strengthened.

All these processes can be assisted through the preparation of short briefing sheets – the *modular specifications* – which conform to a certain standard pattern and provide all the information referred to in the last few pages. The actual format will need to be worked out by each school or team according to its own special needs, but the following blueprint (Figure 6.2) offers a way in which this might be tackled.

The advantages of such a standardised form are that the same criteria are used in considering each module, and that the planner is made aware of the importance of a comprehensive review of the module's development, along with its wider implications. Moreover, comments must be brief and concise – there is not enough room to expand upon ideas at great length!

Figure 6.2   *A Blueprint for Modular Specification*

TITLE .... REF. NO. ....

LENGTH .... STAFF ....

AIMS ....

....

....

OBJECTIVES ....

....

....

....

....

CONTENT ....

....

....

....

METHODOLOGY ....

....

EQUIPMENT .... FACILITIES ....

ASSESSMENT PROCEDURES ....

....

First hand examples

Not all schemes agreee over the composition of the modular specification, nor over the terminology employed. Compare, for example, the specifications required for modular submission by the Northern Partnership for Records of Achievement (Curricular Item 20) and the Cambridgeshire TVEI Consortium's recommended proforma for 'A' level units (Curricular Item 21), with a non-examination module from the Northern Ireland Council for Educational Development (NICED) (Curricular Item 22). NICED made use of the Scottish Action Plan framework to develop this scheme. At present it is a non-examination module, but discussions are taking place about the possibility of GCSE accreditation for the overall scheme from which this extract is taken.

CURRICULAR ITEM 20
Submission of modules

CRITERIA FOR A UNIT OF WORK

a A unit must be a discrete, coherent programme of work which can be assessed.

b The title of the unit must be meaningful to users of the letter of credit.

c The unit submission must
 i specify the curricular area(s) to which the unit relates;

 ii describe the unit briefly in terms of the learning objectives and processes involved, and the educational contexts in which learning will take place;

 iii specify the outcomes which are to be accredited (which must be observable during the process and/or in the product and be clearly related to the unit title and the unit description) in terms of one or more of the following:

 - the abilities or skills which the student will demonstrate
 - the concepts of which the student will acquire an understanding
 - the knowledge which the student will show
 - the processes which the student will experience;

 iv specify the way in which each of the outcomes is to be demonstrated and the evidence of attainment that is to be retained for each outcome for inspection by an assessor;

 v specify the centre's procedures for making and recording assessments.

THE SUBMISSION OF UNITS FOR VALIDATION

Units must be submitted to LEA pre-validating committees and to regional validating committees using both the format and the form of words agreed by the LEAs.

In the unit submission the outcomes to be accredited must be introduced as follows.

 In successfully completing this unit the student will have

 demonstrated the ability to .... (skills)
 acquired an understanding of .... (concepts)

> shown knowledge of ....
> experienced ....

In the unit submission the relationship between each of the intended outcomes of the unit, the evidence of students' achievements to be retained for each outcome and the assessment and recording procedures must be clearly shown by means of numerical cross-reference.

Centres are advised to take great care in specifying in the unit submission the evidence of students' achievements to be retained for inspection by an assessor.

Reproduced by permission of the Northern Partnership for Records of Achievement

CURRICULAR ITEM 21
Modular Specification, Lay-out for TVEI
A level submission

Title	Date	Ref No

Level	(full module/half module)

Type and purpose of module

    (A brief statement indicating broad aims of the module and the probable target audience)

Previous experience necessary
    (If students should have studied other modules before starting this one)

Learning outcomes/assessment objectives

> (Knowledge – principles, language, processes, key ideas etc.
> Skills – diagnose, manipulate data, plan, solve problems etc.
> Attitudes – work co-operatively, work safely etc.)

Content

> (Content will be expressed according to the particular subject involved. In some cases the content will be very specific; in others it will be less so, according to the desired learning outcomes.)

Learning/teaching approaches

> (Working alone/in groups/in pairs/individualised learning
> Team teaching
> Projects/assignments/field study/demonstrations
> Residential/work experience/practical work etc.)

Materials/resources

> (Equipment desired to achieve the assessment objectives and the learning/teaching approaches)

Assessment outlines

> (Related to assessment objectives and the learning/teaching style
>
> Objective tests, short answers, essays, diaries, folders, profiles, reports, orals, case studies, finished products, performance observations etc.)

Assessment relationships

> (The relation of this module's assessment to the total assessment of the subject. Specification Grid.)

Performance levels

> (Some indication of what is considered to be a satisfactory performance in relation to an example paper. Marking scheme. Grading criteria for grades A, B and E.)

Proposals for moderation

Evaluation

Reproduced with permission from: Cambridgeshire TVEI Consortium, *Modular A Level Guidelines*, 1986, pp.15–16.

CURRICULAR ITEM 22
Modular specification

THEME	PERSONAL AND SOCIAL DEVELOPMENT: ESSENTIAL MINIMAL CAPABILITIES
TITLE	AWARENESS OF ENTERPRISE/SELF EMPLOYMENT
ENTRY LEVEL	BASIC: 14–18 years
DURATION	20 hours
RATIONALE	This module is closely linked to the Post-16 Opportunities modules and should be seen as an extension of existing mainstream careers and work experience programmes. It aims to raise awareness among young people about the advantages and disadvantages of self employment.

AIMS	1	**GENERAL**

a **PERSONAL DEVELOPMENT**

Independent thinking, caring and decision-making skills to encourage attitudes such as self-confidence, self-esteem and self-discipline.

b **SOCIAL DEVELOPMENT**

   i Communication skills, inter-personal skills and the capacity for co-operative action.

   ii Group planning and group decision-making skills.

2 **SPECIFIC**

To help young people:

a become aware of self-employment as an option and what self-employment demands at a personal level.

b assess the personal characteristics considered appropriate for self-employment and in doing so

   • become aware of their own positive attributes
   • become aware of their own development needs

c **EITHER**

   i gain insight into the advantages and disadvantages of self-employment through contact with an enterprise centre or a self-employed person

   OR

   ii gain a basic awareness of the business skill of market research

d decide whether or not to explore this option further and if so, identify an appropriate educational/training/employment path.

ASSESSMENT | **GENERAL OBJECTIVES**

This term is used to describe the skills/abilities which are measured and recorded for assessment purposes.

These include skills/abilities which involve:

• recall
• understanding (ie analysis and interpretation)
• processes and decision making (ie evaluation, application, extrapolation)

NB Not all the aims can necessarily be translated readily into assessment objectives but this does not detract from

	their importance in the achievement of the overall aims of the scheme. These should be developed through appropriate teaching and learning approaches.
ASSESSMENT PROCEDURE	**SUMMARY** For formal assessment purposes pupils will be expected to: • submit a short piece of written work • undertake an individual interview of 5–10 minutes • present evidence of a visit/interview or market reseach and a short written summary • participate in group discussion or individual counselling.
SUGGESTED TEACHING AND LEARNING APPROACHES	1 **GENERAL** It is important that teachers, where possible, adopt an experiential rather than a didactic, mode of teaching. Pupils should have opportunities to demonstrate, and act upon, their own initiative. Classroom organisational arrangements should be in keeping with this form of teaching and learning. Teachers should use a balanced variety of whole class, group and individual teaching methods which provide opportunities for pupils • to acquire the information relevant to this module • to acquire practical and other identified skills • to participate in the range of identified school-based and out-of-school experiences • to gain in self-confidence and self-esteem 2 **SPECIFIC** (see Resources List at the end of this module) **Specific Aim 1** • Video and other stimulus material, simulation games and visiting speakers **Specific aim 2** • Groupwork and individual counselling, questionnaires and skills inventories; confidence building exercises and positive discussion **Specific aim 3** • Visits to enterprise centres, to self-employed people in small businesses; interviews, self-presentation; simulation **Specific aim 4** • Group discussion and individual counselling.

Reproduced by permission of the Northern Ireland Council for Educational Development

For further reading

J. White's *The Aims of Education Restated* (Routledge and Kegan Paul, 1982) is one of the few books devoted specifically to this subject.

Objectives and their use in the planning of a curriculum are given good coverage in *How to Help Learners Assess their Progress* by R Lewis (CET, 1985), *A Workshop on the Writing of Learning Objectives* by T J Russell (Coombe Lodge, 1979) and *Objectives in Curricular Design* by I K Davies (McGraw Hill, 1976).

Practical examples are given in *Education for Capability* edited by T Burgess (NFER/Nelson, 1985) and discussion of how the needs of the less able can be met in this way is found in *Preventing Classroom Failure* by M Ainslow and D A Tweddle (Wiley, 1979).

7 Motivation through Modules

Care needs to be taken not only in the planning and preparation of modules, and the manner in which they combine to form a programme, but over the initial presentation of the scheme to the students. The power of such units to motivate begins at this point, and first impressions are always important. All the work described in the last two chapters could go for nothing if the full potential of the scheme is not made clear to all concerned; if the opportunities it unlocks do not come across. No amount of preparation, however painstaking, or modular linkages, however astute, can hope to make up for an inadequate or uninformed selection at this – or at any – stage in the procedure.

Selecting the modules

Many schools approach the selection process through a booklet, or information sheet, which sets out in a few sentences the nature of each module and describes clearly the principles, if any, to be adopted in building up programmes of work. These details are then studied by the pupils either during an appropriate lesson or within tutorial groupings. The advantage of the former is that, if the scheme is departmentally planned, those who have prepared modules can be on hand to answer questions relating to them. The whole scheme can also be presented to the pupils together, either by the Departmental Head or key personnel within that section of the school.

The personal tutor, on the other hand, be this within a House or a Year grouping, may well be in a better position to know precisely what is being studied by each individual across the curriculum and might thus be better placed to give advice of a more general nature. Some schools combine both these features and appoint specialist teachers from subjects offering such courses who can be available at tutorial time to fill in with more background detail. The overall scheme, presented in as simple a form as possible, should be displayed in the main Departmental areas and in the school library.

Just how effective directness of approach and simplicity of format can be in getting information across is amply illustrated in Curricular Item 23, from Hemsworth High School.

CURRICULAR ITEM 23: Getting the Message Across
Hemsworth High School, Yorkshire

The Unit:

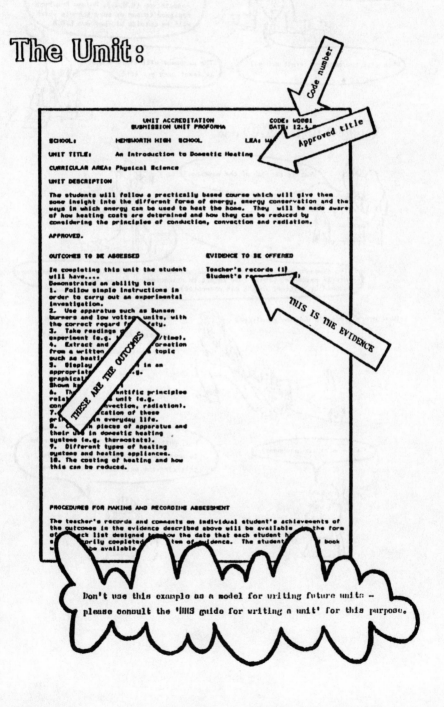

Code number

Approved title

UNIT ACCREDITATION
SUBMISSION UNIT PROFORMA

CODE: WO001
DATE: 12.1

SCHOOL: HEMSWORTH HIGH SCHOOL

LEA: WA

UNIT TITLE: An Introduction to Domestic Heating

CURRICULAR AREA: Physical Science

UNIT DESCRIPTION

The students will follow a practically based course which will give them some insight into the different forms of energy, energy conservation and the ways in which energy can be used to heat the home. They will be made aware of how heating costs are determined and how they can be reduced by considering the principles of conduction, convection and radiation.

APPROVED.

OUTCOMES TO BE ASSESSED

In completing this unit the student will have....
Demonstrated an ability to:
1. Follow simple instructions in order to carry out an experimental investigation.
2. Use apparatus such as Bunsen burners and low voltage units, with the correct regard f fety.
3. Take readings /time).
experiment (e.g.
4. Extract and ormation
from a written topic
such as heati
5. Display in an
appropriat .g.
graphical
Shown k
6. The antific principles
rela unit (e.g.
con nvection, radiation).
7. cation of these
pri n everyday life.
8. C h pieces of apparatus and
their u in domestic heating
system (e.g. thermostats).
9. Different types of heating systems and heating appliances.
10. The costing of heating and how this can be reduced.

EVIDENCE TO BE OFFERED

Teacher's records (1)
Student's re   )

THESE ARE THE OUTCOMES

THIS IS THE EVIDENCE

PROCEDURES FOR MAKING AND RECORDING ASSESSMENT

The teacher's records and comments on individual student's achievements of the outcomes in the evidence described above will be available the form
of ck list designed to ow the date that each student h
a orily completed tem of idence. The student book
w be available

Don't use this example as a model for writing future units —
please consult the 'UIIS guide for writing a unit' for this purpose.

This is material evidence (written work, constructions, videos etc.) that an outcome has been achieved which the assessor will actually be able to see on assessment day.

This is evidence for an outcome which cannot be supported by primary evidence (e.g. outcome: "the ability to follow instructions"). Normally a teacher's record/record sheet would be used as 'secondary evidence'.

This is a written record (dated and signed) with comments stating that a particular outcome has been achieved. It is best used as SECONDARY EVIDENCE.

...Questions

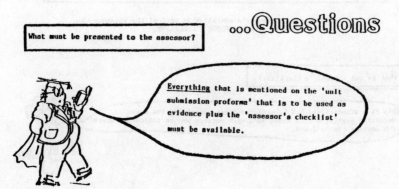

Everything that is mentioned on the 'unit submission proforma' that is to be used as evidence plus the 'assessor's checklist' must be available.

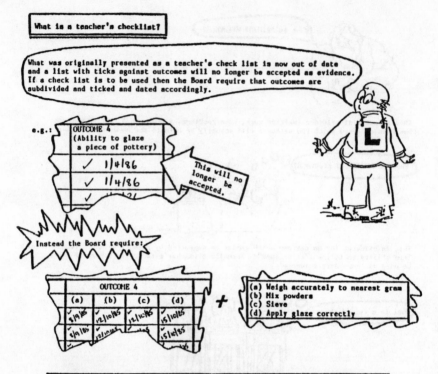

What is a teacher's checklist?

What was originally presented as a teacher's check list is now out of date and a list with ticks against outcomes will no longer be accepted as evidence. If a check list is to be used then the Board require that outcomes are subdivided and ticked and dated accordingly.

e.g.:

OUTCOME 4
(Ability to glaze
a piece of pottery)

✓ 1/4/86
✓ 1/4/86

This will no longer be accepted.

Instead the Board require:

OUTCOME 4			
(a)	(b)	(c)	(d)
5/9/85	12/10/85	12/10/85	15/10/85
5/9/86	12/10/85		15/10/85

+

(a) Weigh accurately to nearest gram
(b) Mix powders
(c) Sieve
(d) Apply glaze correctly

Many teachers may find this modification problematic so the advice is either DON'T USE A CHECKLIST AS PART OF YOUR EVIDENCE or modify your existing check list accordingly. (NB all new units which have a checklist as part of the evidence will have to include the checklist for approval with the unit itself).

If your unit contains a teacher's checklist as part of the evidence then this will now be replaced by an ASSESSOR'S CHECKLIST.

What is the Assessor's Checklist?

This is a standardized H.H.S. produced sheet containing the names of successful pupils, a tick along side each outcome and an indication where each outcome can be found.

Hemsworth High School
UNIT ACCREDITATION

ASSESSOR'S CHECKLIST

| Unit title | Code number |

| Name | Outcomes |

To produce your assessor's checklist:-
(1) obtain a H.H.S. school proforma:

| Outcome description | where evidence can be found |

Teacher ....

Date ....

Hemsworth High School
UNIT ACCREDITATION

(2) fill it in as follows:

ASSESSOR'S CHECKLIST

Unit title AN INTRODUCTION TO DOMESTIC HEATING   Code number WD001

Name	Outcomes									
	1	2	3	4	5	6	7	8	9	10

Eventually enter here the names, **in alphabetical order** (boys/girls), of only the successful students.

Each outcome should be ticked and/or dated for each student.

Outcome description

In completing this unit the student will have....
Demonstrated an ability to:
1. Follow simple instructions in order to carry out an experimental investigation.
2. ... apparatus such as Bunsen burners, voltage units, with the ... for safety.
3. ... (time).
...
such ...
5. Display ... appropriate ... graphically.
Shown knowledge of:
6. The basic scientific ... relating to this unit (e.g. conduction, convection, radiation).
7. The application of these principles in everyday life.
8. Certain pieces of apparatus and their use in domestic heating systems (e.g. thermostats).
9. Different types of heating systems and heating appliances.
10. The costing of heating and how this can be reduced.

This section could be cut or copied from the approved Unit submission sheet.

where evidence can be found

The teacher's record will be evidence of outcome (1), all the other outcomes will be indicated with the appropriate number as they occur in the students' note books.

(3) This can now be copied in sufficient quantities for future requirements.

Teacher ....   Date ....

Prior to the Submission of Material for ....

Just where are those outcomes ?

.... Assessment

In an attempt to make future visits of the assessor straight forward and more rewarding for our students, the following suggestions are being made.

(i) do NOT rely on the dating of work as a means of finding outcomes - this also makes retrospective entry difficult.

(ii) when marking the work **indicate with the outcome number where that outcome has been achieved.**

(iii) get the students to number all their pages and rule up a summary chart on the inside cover along the following lines: (the students will keep this up to date)

OUTCOME NUMBER	PAGE/TITLE OF WORK SHEET WHERE OUTCOME IS ACHIEVED
1	
2	
3	

This will act also as an 'at a glance' pass or fail checklist.

EVERY UNIT SUBMITTED FOR ASSESSMENT MUST NOW HAVE AN "ASSESSOR'S CHECKLIST".

Some staff have produced booklets for their unit, these have been very easy to assess and examples, along with advice, are available if other staff wish to do likewise.

Contrasting approaches

An interesting contrast in the approach adopted to modular selection is
provided by the two Departments from *Peers School, Oxford*, cited in
Case Studies Eight and Nine. Both achieve cohesion of content within
diversity of choice, but go about it in rather different ways.

Community Studies (see Case Study Eight) places a lot of emphasis
upon an interlocking set of *cores* and *options*, with specific paths through
them being mapped out beforehand and clearly 'signposted' for the benefit
of different groups. Advice is always available, from individual subject
teachers, Heads of subsidiary sections or the school's pastoral system.
But the overall direction of the work is laid down within certain paramet-
ers; what is sacrificed in flexibility of units or freedom of choice is more
than compensated for by internal cohesiveness of content within what
remains a relatively open system.

The major problems that could arise in schemes such as this are a
failure of individual members of staff fully to comprehend the complete
range of choices available to students, or undue pressure being brought
to bear on individuals by one or more of the curricular dimensions.

There are no 'core' modules within the *Science and Technology* Department, where even the different units that contribute towards GCSE may
normally be followed in any order. Great store is here set by freedom of
individual choice, but *subject tutors* are nominated to ensure that students
are fully aware of what is available to them and that an informed, sensible
selection of modules actually takes place. Here there is plenty of guidance
for individuals through a plethora of units but no certainty for those
teaching them that certain pieces of background information will be
known, or that they can rely on a unified corporate body of knowledge
among those taking the module.

Each approach has its own strengths and weaknesses. But they share
a belief that the overall scheme should be fully comprehended not only
by those who are going either to teach or to learn through it, but by the
rest of the staff as well.

It is not always possible, for staffing and timetabling reasons, to have
the full complement of modules always available for student choice. One
solution might be an extensive use of modular banking (see page 102)
where a large number of units is kept permanently on file. Over the years
a hundred or more modules could be put at the school's disposal, to be
brought out as and when required. Another, more common approach is
to ensure, through careful blocking and timetabling procedures, that
during the course of the year each student has access to a complete
cross-section of curricular choice. This, combined with strong tutorial
support, is a feature of Ysgol Emrys ap Iwan, the Welsh school first
encountered in Case Study Seven.

CURRICULAR ITEM 24: Facilitating modular choice and balance, Ysgol Emrys ap Iwan

ADDITIONAL STUDIES MODULES AVAILABLE

MONDAYS and TUESDAYS

ART	1
COMPUTER PROGRAMMING	1
DRAMA	1
ELECTRONICS	1
FRENCH	1
HOME MANAGEMENT & LOOKING AFTER YOURSELF	
INTERVIEW TECHNIQUES	
INTRODUCTION TO COMPUTING	1
INFORMATION SYSTEMS	1
LEISURE	
MASS MEDIA	1
MUSIC	1
PHOTOGRAPHY	
TECHNICAL GRAPHIC ART	
TV PRODUCTION	
TYPEWRITING	1
WORD PROCESSING	1

THURSDAYS and FRIDAYS

BIOLOGICAL SCIENCE	1
COMPUTERS IN BUSINESS	
ELECTRONICS	1
ELECTRONIC MUSIC	
HOME MAINTENANCE	
HOME MANAGEMENT & LOOKING AFTER YOURSELF	
INTERVIEW TECHNIQUES	
INTRODUCTION TO COMPUTING	
INFORMATION SYSTEMS	1
LEISURE	
MASS MEDIA	1
PHOTOGRAPHY	
PRACTICAL OFFICE SKILLS	1
PSYCHOLOGY	
ROBOTICS	1
TV PRODUCTION	
TYPEWRITING	
WORD PROCESSING	1

ART	1 & 2
DRAMA	1 & 2
COMPUTER PROGRAMMING	1 & 2
ELECTRONICS	1 & 2
FRENCH	1 & 2
HOME GARDENING	
INFORMATION SYSTEMS	1 & 2
INTERVIEW TECHNIQUES	
LEISURE	
MASS MEDIA	1 & 2
MUSIC	2
PHOTOGRAPHY	
TECHNICAL GRAPHIC ART	
TOURISM	
TV PRODUCTION	
TYPEWRITING	1 & 2
WORD PROCESSING	1

BIOLOGICAL SCIENCE	2
COMMUNITY RELATIONS	
COMPUTER GRAPHIC	
COMPUTER PROGRAMMING	1 & 2
ELECTRONICS	1 & 2
ELECTRONIC MUSIC	
HOME MAINTENANCE	
INFORMATION SYSTEMS	1 & 2
INTERVIEW TECHNIQUES	
LEISURE	
MASS MEDIA	1 & 2
PHOTOGRAPHY	
PRACTICAL OFFICE SKILLS	1 & 2
PSYCHOLOGY	
ROBOTICS	2
TOURISM	
TV PRODUCTION	
TYPEWRITING	1 & 2
WORD PROCESSING	1

PLUS OTHER MODULES AS REQUIRED

CURRICULAR ITEM 24 (continued)

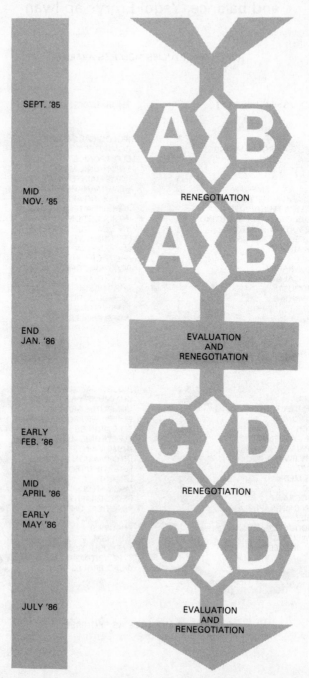

SEPT. '85

MID
NOV. '85

RENEGOTIATION

END
JAN. '86

EVALUATION
AND
RENEGOTIATION

EARLY
FEB. '86

MID
APRIL '86

RENEGOTIATION

EARLY
MAY '86

JULY '86

EVALUATION
AND
RENEGOTIATION

Reproduced with permission from S. Pyart *Modules in Action: A School's Experience*, Ysgol Emrys ap Iwan, pp.14–15

Consulting the parents

It is important that parents are brought into this process of modular selection as early as possible. Special evenings can be arranged at which full documentation is available and at which there is plenty of time to ask questions. Parents might well be drawn in to help with certain modules if their interest is kindled in this way and, of course, the modular approach is ideal for building in short-term commitment of this kind. Pupils take home the modular sheets shortly after this, or even beforehand, and so adequate consultation is ensured.

In schemes where a specific combination of modules is required, much time and anxiety can be saved if sheets are prepared which set out quite clearly the options and then require either ticks or crosses in the appropriate boxes. The simpler these sheets are the better, and there is now nothing to stop such information being transferred directly onto a microprocessor. In schools where Computer Studies is well advanced, or in Departments of Mathematics, this could be done by the pupils themselves, the processor being programmed not to accept non-valid choices. Such a system would give instant information on the take-up of various modules, who had chosen them, and the track-record of different students through a course or modules within a scheme.

All these points are brought together in Case Study 13, a sheet prepared by Ysgol Emrys ap Iwan. This should be read in conjunction with Case Study 7 and Curricular Item 5 (on pages 53 and 29 respectively).

CASE STUDY THIRTEEN
Communication and Consultation at Ysgol Emrys ap Iwan

Negotiation

Negotiation at the end of the third year for 14+ courses is a major undertaking in most secondary schools. The modular curriculum increases the frequency of negotiation but may decrease the importance of any one curriculum decision made by the pupils. At Ysgol Emrys ap Iwan efforts are made, through meetings with parents and pupils, to explain fully the structure, benefits and pitfalls of a modular system involving 470 fourth and fifth years. Modular systems are not operating in the neighbouring 11–18 schools and parents are naturally concerned to discuss the implications for their children. At the end of the third year pupils choose four modules, two of which they will actually follow during the first nine weeks of their fourth year. Two new modules are selected every nine weeks during the fourth year and parents are provided with forms and information to assist their children in making a choice. A total of eight modules are completed in the fourth year. During the fifth year it is necessary for students to complete GCSE courses, so a period of a week at the end of the fourth year is set aside for staff/parent/student negotiations over planning the modules to be completed in the following year. Limitations on staffing and group size dictate this rationalisation of the negotiation procedures.

Any one choice of module is not as important as the selection of an option for both fourth and fifth year but choice of modules is still an important event requiring advice and information. The system has been partly designed to allow students freedom to choose a stand-alone module on the grounds of its intrinsic interest. It would be impossible for any student to choose a completely disconnected set of modules because there are so many ways in which they feed into City and Guilds 365. A few of the more able students felt that only certain courses have credibility and that too many students are just 'doing the modules' without any meaningful aim. The evidence suggests, however, that following courses for their own sake without a recognised qualification at the end does not appeal to the majority of students.

Most pupils felt that sufficient guidance was given over choice of modules. Many relied on their parents for help, or on informal meetings with key teaching staff. The negotiation period at the end of the fourth year was viewed as very valuable by the students. It appeared that some welcomed the opportunity to settle on their remaining six modules. Though they were still selecting some stand-alone modules they felt more secure that they would be able to complete examination courses. A few students were worried that the pressure on certain modules might mean that they could not complete a course. A minority were disappointed over their choice but this concerned stand-alone modules only such as Russian for a student committed to 10 examination courses already.

The organisation of the modules is a mammoth task requiring a great deal of teacher time. The negotiation of the choice with students is shared by several teachers, one of whom has responsibility for organising the modular curriculum with the school's timetabler. This role is very demanding,as the needs and interests of so many students must be satisfied within a fairly rigid structure.

Any significant breakdown in the system could be damaging to the esteem in which the modular curriculum is held. Students had confidence generally that their wishes would be met. A certain amount of flexibility had to be built into the system including teachers who could offer a number of modules and fluid timetabling which allowed extra modules to be included.

Negotiation is a major feature of the project work involved in most modular courses. Teachers concerned with guiding project work may not know the individual students as well as in an option system because they may have taught them for only one module. Project guidelines have been produced to assist students and staff in organising projects.

Reproduced with permission from: S. Pyart, *Evaluating a Modular Curriculum*, Ysgol Emrys ap Iwan, pp. 34–36.

Options – open or closed?

Choice between modules within a scheme may be completely open – that is, entry to them is available to anyone within a given age group. In other cases choice may be restricted by the entry requirements of certain modules; for example, they may use language or terminology comprehensible only under particular circumstances or at a certain stage in a course. Clearly, it is important to differentiate carefully between the two 'types' of module. For instance, Curricular Item 25 is the description of a 'closed' module which is perfectly acceptable as part of a stratified, or even sequential, scheme, but would mean little to the average pupil.

CURRICULAR ITEM 25
Module within Stratified Scheme

COURSE UNIT NUMBER: 6

TITLE: BLOOD AND CIRCULATION

DURATION: 3 WEEKS

KEY CONCEPTS	RELATIONSHIP BETWEEN VOLUME AND SURFACE AREA NEED FOR AN INTERNAL TRANSPORT SYSTEM CONTINUITY OF THE BODY'S FLUID SYSTEMS ADVANTAGE OF A PARALLEL CIRCUIT IMMUNITY

PRACTICAL SKILLS	MAKING A BLOOD SLIDE INTERPRETING A SLIDE OR PHOTOMICROGRAPH

FACTUAL KNOWLEDGE	THE STRUCTURE AND FUNCTIONS OF BLOOD DOUBLE CIRCULATION SYSTEM STRUCTURE OF HEART AND HEART CYCLE LYMPHATIC SYSTEM

CURRICULAR ITEM 25 (continued)

ASSESSMENT	QUALITY OF BLOOD SLIDE (WORKSHEET 60)
	RESPONSES TO BIOSTRIP 96
	UNIT TEST ON BLOOD AND CIRCULATION
	HOMEWORK ON WORKSHEET 59

Reproduced by permission of Thomas Tallis School, London.

No mistake should be made about modules in a genuinely open system. Their descriptions are for the pupils, not for the staff; there should be no ambiguity concerning the title. Here, for example, are some modular titles culled from a variety of schemes. How easy is it to tell what the subject matter will be? *Angers to Jumpers; The Agony and the Ecstasy; Furious Forties; Flights of Fancy.*

Describing a module

Curricular Item 26 is the description of another module this time from Ysgol Emrys ap Iwan (see page 143). This has all the hallmarks of a unit which is genuinely open. It is written in simple terms, addressed directly to the student, contains no technical language or 'in-terminology' and is completely free-standing.

CURRICULAR ITEM 26
Free-Standing and Open Module

TOURISM

Tourism is a major industry in Wales. Over the United Kingdom as a whole employment in tourism-related industries – hotel and catering, sport, entertainment, retailing – is estimated at over one and a half million jobs. In this module a brief history of tourism in the Borough of Colwyn forms the starting point. The theme is then developed by studying tourism today in this area; a purpose-built tourist area in Scotland; and a tourist area in Spain. Using brochures and 'fact-sheets', costings and travel are discussed in relation to holidays. Visits to (a) an official dealing with tourism in this area; (b) a director of a major tourist attraction; (c) an hotelier who has served on the Wales Tourist Board and (d) a caravan site locally, form an integral part of the course.

Reproduced with permission from S. Pyart, *Modules in Action: A School's Experience*, Ysgol Emrys ap Iwan, Appendix 4.

Other units are described entirely in terms of what is to be done. This makes them both attractive and explicable, as Curricular Item 27, from Peers School, Oxford, illustrates.

CURRICULAR ITEM 27
Free-Standing Module written in Behavioural Terms

Target – Foundation

Pupil's skills: The course is designed to provide you with the skills necessary to:

1 Wire a normal household 3-pin plug
2 Know the purpose of a fuse and how fuse boxes (and MCB) function
3 Have a basic knowledge of how modern ring main circuits are set out and wired, through building low-voltage models
4 Read a domestic electricity meter and calculate the amount of electricity used and so check your bills are correct
5 Know how various domestic appliances work eg, immersion heaters
6 Reduce your (electrical) energy consumption through insulation and careful use of electricity
7 Use electricity safely in the home

Reproduced by permission of Peers School, Oxford.

Sharing the information

In compiling short details of a unit to facilitate student choice, the modular specification outlined on page 125 could be of great help. Obviously not all the information here will be of value to the student, but many schools like to share as much as possible with them before a final choice is made (see Curricular Item 28).

Some schemes incorporate a contract into the process of modular selection. This can be written at varying levels of formality and indicates the major undertakings involved should the module be selected. This system of positively contracting in, rather than the more negative one of opting out or 'voting with one's feet' is common in further education. Other schemes set out to establish the kind of interaction between teacher and pupil advocated by David Hargreaves in Chapter 1 (see page 7). Such interaction is, of course, by no means unique to modular planning, but the short duration of the units and the clear goals established for each make it particularly appropriate. Nowhere is this more clearly

CURRICULAR ITEM 28
Modular Specification for Student Choice

ART DEPARTMENT 1.5.5

UNIT ONE .... **WORKING FROM OBJECTS**

In this unit we will be working from objects. We are trying to encourage you to look more closely, to develop your skills in drawing in a variety of different media/materials and approaches.

Objectives:

1   To develop the ability to use drawing as a means of recording, describing, and understanding the appearance of things seen.
2   To convey information about how things work (industrial), how things grow (organic).
3   To make personal responses to things seen.
4   To recognise the potential for developing work in other 2D/3D units and other areas of curriculum.

Organisation of the unit:

To include work on the following 'basic elements':

LINE, TONE, TEXTURE, COLOUR

Week 1-3:

Selection of objects natural and industrial, emphasising contrast.
Detailed observation of above: a Linear
                                                     b Textural
                                                     c Tonal
Using some or all of the following materials:
pencil, charcoal, pastels, ink, collage, crayons etc.

Weeks 4–6:

Colour studies of objects

Personal interpretation.
Using paint, collage, pastel, ink etc.

demonstrated than when modules are 'banked' – prepared by an individual or group and then placed on file to be used at a later date should the need arise.

Banking on success

As has been seen, it is unlikely that banked modules will be taught by those who prepared them, and so great emphasis is usually placed on what the pupils are required to do, with as much information as possible being made available to help them. Teachers presenting such modules frequently work in an advisory or tutorial capacity, being on hand to answer questions as and when they arise and to ensure that the work runs smoothly. They are the highly professional facilitators and managers of the learning process. The ingenuity and attention to detail displayed by those who write the material in the first place will help enormously here. The banked module presented in Curricular Item 29 exemplifies a full range of exercises devised not merely as highly participative in their own right, but also to draw out the precise points that are required to fulfil the central aims and objectives of the unit.

CURRICULAR ITEM 29
A Banked Module – 'Looking at Newspapers'

1 *History of the press*
Tape/slide sequence; prepared text; library research; resource material; class work

2 *Today's newspapers*
Copies of daily press; workcards; resource material; group and class work; questionnaire

3 *Analysis of press*
Copies of papers; analysis sheet; worksheets; individual and group research; class work

4 *Writing a story*
Workcard; library research; individual and group work

5 *Photojournalism*
Video(s); newspapers; individual/group work

6 *Censorship*
Analysis sheet; individual work; class discussion

7 *The local press*
Copies of local newspapers; vist to newspaper office; individual and group work

8 *Doing it for real*
Simulation; resource pack

Examples from a variety of sources and subject areas can be used to illustrate the principles involved.

Assignments

In Curricular Item 30, an assignment item from a banked module,the roles of both teacher and pupil are clearly defined within this item, with by far the greater emphasis being placed upon active learning and the reaching of independent conclusions. At specific points in this and other modules in the series, the pupils are instructed to 'consult your teacher', 'ask advice', and so on. Great care has to be taken by those preparing the unit to list all the resources and equipment required, and by those teaching it to ensure that such materials are made available from the outset. The main focus is on the really important aspects of the module, the conducting of experiments and recording of results, and directions are explicit concerning routine elements such as setting up the equipment. The teacher can now spend more time on professional activities, such as helping individuals and giving encouragement, while each student proceeds more or less at his own pace.

In writing these modules it is important that the results of experiments are not revealed or the answers supplied in advance. The structure should, however, direct the pupils' attention to the correct areas and provide a framework within which each can appear to succeed by his own efforts. At the same time it should give progressive training in skills requisite to the subject being followed.

Even in highly creative areas, the overall purpose of each unit must be made clear, but this needs to be done in a manner which opens up – rather than closes down – opportunities for discussion, questioning and reaching independent conclusions. Indeed, it is the reaching of a conclusion that has meaning for the individual that is important, rather than arriving at a single 'right' answer; it makes the outcome of such units – to use Eisner's phrase – 'expressive'.

Discussion

The above point is well brought out by the way discussion is handled. Emphasis is often placed on the role of the chairman, with the late Lawrence Stenhouse's concept of that person's neutrality frequently being cited.[1] Stenhouse also placed great emphasis on provision of the right kind of material so that a balanced view might be gained, preventing such exercises from degenerating into a mere 'pooling of ignorance'!

The Newspaper Unit takes this even further and bases discussion as far as possible on real-life situations. The item on Censorship is a case in point (Curricular Item 31).

---

[1]   See Stenhouse, L. *An Introduction to Curriculum Research and Development* (Heinemann, 1975).

CURRICULAR ITEM 30
Assignment Item from Banked Module

AIR : HEATING AND BURNING

1. Cover the lighted candles as shown. Time how long each takes to go out.

_____ sec   _____ sec   _____ sec   _____ sec

Now try to explain this _____

---

2. Using this equipment find out what
   happens when the stoppered tube is
   placed over the candle.
   What happens to the candle flame?

   _____

   What happens to the water level
   inside the tube?

   _____

   _____

   Is air 'used up' in burning? _____

3.

Light the candle and cover with the bell
jar. What happens to the balloon?

At first? _____

After a time? _____

What happens to the water level?

At first? _____

After a time? _____

---

4. Heat this equipment. Is the tube

   empty? _____

   What do you see? _____

   Why is this? _____

   _____

   Let the tube cool. What happens?

   _____

   Why should we normally remove the
   delivery tube from the water?

   _____

   _____

CURRICULAR ITEM 30 (continued)

5.

bulldog clip
on stand.

metre rule

plastic bag
or tin can

candle held under
bag or tin on one side.

Set up this equipment.   Keep the flame
about 20cm from the bag.   CAREFUL.
What happens to the bag which has been

heated? _____

What could we say warm air tends to do?

_____

Now see your teacher.

Reproduced by permission of Mr.G. Moore

CURRICULAR ITEM 31
Banked Item as preparation for Discussion

CENSORSHIP

You are the editor of a highly popular daily newspaper, with control over everything that goes into it. The following items have been passed by the Legal Department, but which of them would you allow to appear?

a   Under three columns indicate which you would definitely sanction, which you would refuse to print, and which you would take further advice over.

b   Put the items in rank order, No 1 being the least objectionable and No 10 being the most offensive.

c   Be prepared to discuss your reasons for these judgements.

1   Photograph of member of Royal family sunbathing in nude.

2   Advertisement: 'Drunk as a Lord; Free as the Wind' – potion to deceive breathaliser yet allow you to continue to drink.

3   Article: Full and Frank Confessions of an Unrepentant Dope-Peddlar.

4   Interview with grief-stricken father of girl who has been raped.

CURRICULAR ITEM 31 (continued)

5 Leading Article: 'First the Suez Fiasco: Now the Debacle of Malvinos'.

6 Feature article revealing that leading politician was a member of the Communist Party at age 17.

7 Do-it-yourself strip cartoon illustrating how to make a molotov cocktail.

8 The obscene words of the latest Punk hit.

9 A favourable review of a film featuring sex with children.

10 Headline and page 1 spot: 'They Take our Jobs; They take our Women; They take our Homes; Now make them Take the First Boat Home'.

11 Interview with leader of IRA Bomb Squad operating undercover in Britain.

12 Contingency plans for evacuating major cities in case of nuclear war.

Audio visual aids

Slides, filmstrips or even video recordings may be used by groups or individuals on their own, as well as being presented to the whole class. In this case, the teacher will probably wish to prepare notes to go with the material, relating it directly to the unit being followed. Filmstrips may well be cut into individual frames and separately mounted for this purpose. Another approach is to create a complete, well-indexed library of all such visual material which can then be used in a far more flexible manner as and when the need arises.

Use of library

It is to be hoped that the requisite skills, such as lay-out of the library, Dewey system, using reference material and the indexing of material within a text, will have been part of a study skills programme (see page 47). If not, then a brief introduction to them will be necessary.

Outside visits

These need to be carefully prepared, with both group and host organisation knowing precisely what is the purpose and what the group should gain from such a visit. Workcards or sheets may be used in conjunction with outside visits.

Questionnaires

Curricular Item 32 indicates quite clearly how classroom work and the principles relating to most subjects may be drawn from such first-hand evidence if carefully structured.

CURRICULAR ITEM 32
The Use of Questionnaires in Banked Modules, Hemsworth High School

Questionnaire

Do you live in a detatched or semidetatched house
or bungalow?   _____
How many bedrooms?   _____
Do you have loft insulation?   _____
Do you have cavity wall insulation?   _____
Do you have double glazing?   _____
Do you have draught proofing?   _____
What other methods do you have of saving heat?
_____

Do you have central heating, if so, is it gas, electric,
oil or solid fuel?   _____
How do you heat up your hot water?   _____
How do you heat your living room?   _____
How many radiators do you have?   _____
What temperature do you keep your house at?   _____
How much does a ton of coal cost?   _____
How much does a unit of electricity cost?   _____
How much does a therm of gas cost?   _____
What is the cost of heating oil?   _____
Your annual cost for heating your house will be   _____
Do you think this is excessive?   _____
How do you suggest that you could reduce this amount?
_____
_____

Reproduced with permission from: *Keeping Warm: An Introduction to Domestic Heating*, Hemsworth High School, 1986.

CURRICULAR ITEM 33
The Use of Analysis Sheets in Banked Module

Analysis of the Daily Mirror. Tuesday October 6th

	Classification	Example	No.
	News		
(A)	Crime	Girl, 11, is buried alive	11
(B)	Politics	How Mrs Thatcher had kept her cool during a week of commonwealth talks	11
(C)	Social	Jim Davidson and his new bride leaving for their honeymoon.	31
D)	Overseas	Pan Am are cutting their fares from New York to London.	16
(E)	Financial	£30,000 was won from a bingo game	12
(F)	Sport	Snookers pot of gold	24
	Opinion		
(1)	Leading Article	Geoffrey Howe should he be Chancellor?	5
(2)	Critics	A report on Peter Wilson of the mirror	3
(3)	Letters	A woman told of her friendship with her former husband and asked if it was right	10
	Features	Lynne Frederick talked about former husband Peter Sellers	6
	Advertisements	Bilson Head phones	8
			137

Each student was given a copy of one of the newspapers for that day then asked to choose one story from each of the ten categories and to cut out an advertisement that appealed to them. They were also asked to count the stories which came under each heading.

CURRICULAR ITEM 33 (continued)

Our Newspapers analysed.
Graph to show percentages
of articles in each newspaper

PAPER	DATE	ANALYSIS						OPINION			FEATURES	ADVERTS
		A	B	C	D	E	F	1	2	3		
The Times	2.11.81	5	18	16	28	23	50	2	10	12	6	3 pages
Farnham Herald	9.9.81	25	-	-	-	16	30	0.8	9	24	1	18 "
The Star	15.4.81	9	8	19	0.3	5	32	1	1	49	3	8 "
Daily Mail	10.9.81	5	16	18	12	11	18	5	5	10	9	13 "
The Mirror	6.10.81	14	14	41	21	16	17.5	7	4	13	8	8 "
The Sun	22.4.81	10	7	19	4	7	15	3	9	15	13	11 "
The Standard	7.9.81	1	6	21	8	8	12	1	0	6	1	16 "
Daily Express	9.9.81	12	16	15	6	6	20	1	3	7	9	8 "
Daily Telegraph	1.9.81	10	18	8	7	13	11	3	4	11	5	7 "
The Guardian	1.9.81	10	24	36	31	21	37	14	12	21	18	4.5 "
Sunday People	6.9.81	2	2	6	1	2	14	2	0	4	4	6 "

Later, each individual contributed to an overall analysis of the press, from which much discussion ensued.

Structured reading

Sections from textbooks or other material (as long as use is not precluded by copyright), may also be incorporated into a banked module.

Simulation

Here can be incorporated a range of activities – case-studies, role-play, in-tray exercises, games, psycho-drama, etc, which attempt to place individuals or groups in 'other peoples' shoes', to make the work less vicarious or to remove emotional/subjective judgements entailed when giving one's own point of view.

Analysis sheets

These are very useful in basing discussion or research on first-hand evidence rather than hearsay. The Newspaper Module, for example (see page 157), used this approach for finding out exactly what the content of each paper was, how much space was devoted to various elements and how papers compared on this score (see Curricular Item 33).

This approach has been extensively developed by distance-learning agencies, such as the Open University and the National Extension College, from whom important lessons may be learnt. Of especial interest is the 'signalling' of such student-centred activities through a series of symbols, such as those shown in Curricular Item 34. If adopted by a school, such symbols could become a feature of all modular work, their meaning being understood across the curriculum as a whole.

CURRICULAR ITEM 34
The use of symbols in National Extension College units

[S] At the beginning of each unit, you will find a list of study *aims or objectives*; we call them *signposts* to the unit. They tell you what you should be able to do by the end of the unit. They are also useful as a checklist, to make certain you have understood all the essential points when you look back over a unit. You may have found other points you wish to add, and we have left a space for this.

[?] Each unit has some *self-check or review questions*. These usually come at the end of a section, and are intended to enable you to check for yourself that you have understood what you have just read. So often we can nod contentedly over several pages and wake up to read on without noticing what we have missed. Like the signposts, they act as pointers to the more important ideas in the unit, so you will find that it pays to stop reading when you come to a question and write down your answers to it. My answers are printed at the end of each unit and I hope you will find them useful to check against yours. These questions should help you to work on your own, but if you find you still don't understand something which seems important, your tutor will help you work it out.

[A] The third element that you will meet is the *activity*. This does not mean anything strenuous; it is a chance to stop and think, and to reflect on what you have read. Activities suggest tasks for you to do at home, which are designed to increase your understanding, and to help you put new ideas into perspective, using your own experience. In most cases no one will see your answer unless you want to show it to them, so the effort you put into these is entirely up to you. I believe they are useful for students who don't have the benefit of discussion and working with others. Because they take the place of class discussion, most activities don't have a 'right answer', but once again you will find my answer, based on my own experience, at the end of the unit to compare with yours.

[H] There is no single book which, by itself, covers all the topics of the 'A'-level Sociology syllabus. We have chosen M. Haralambos, *Sociology: Themes and Perspectives* (University Tutorial Press, Slough, 1980) as *essential reading* for the course, because we think it provides a valuable summary of many of the basic points. You will need to buy this book, as you will be asked to study examples from it as part of your course work.

[R] The course materials include a *reader*, which is a collection of articles on various aspects of sociology. Our aim in making this collection is to give you a brief taste of the many ways of writing about subjects of sociological interest, and to make easily available to you a greater variety of work than you would have from using only the set book.

Reproduced with permission from P. Henderson, *Sociology A Level, Units 1–7*, NEC, 1981, pp.5–6.

Under some schemes, even greater responsibility devolves upon the students for devising, running and evaluating modular programmes. We turn to these in Chapter 8.

For further reading

Of the few books which bear directly on the content of this chapter, J Haysom's *Inquiry into Teaching Processes* (Ontario Institute for Educational Studies, 1985), the FEU's *Towards a Personal Guidance Base* (1984) and I K Davies' *Management of Learning* (McGraw Hill, 1971) are all worthy of note.

8 Participative Pathways

Four of the dangers associated with the pre-specification of objectives along the lines so far suggested are neatly summarised by Hemsworth High, a school which has had more experience than most in modular planning. These are:

- emphasis upon 'those aspects of learning that are more easily demonstrated';
- the belief sometimes held that 'if an outcome is not included in a unit it cannot be taught';
- 'students and staff 'chasing' outcomes' so that 'accreditation dominates the educational process';
- reluctance 'to give credit for outcomes that are more abstract or expressive in nature'.[1]

The warning is timely. If care is not taken then a kind of modular 'tunnel vision' can develop in which creativity or divergent approaches are sacrificed in an eagerness to arrive at the agreed destination along well-beaten tracks.

Schools usually take positive steps to obviate such excesses while still preserving the very real benefits of criteria-referencing. Here much depends upon the nature of each scheme. Hemsworth, for example, believes that 'It is misleading to regard a unit as a total educational package. It must be seen for what it is, a selection of elements from within a course'. The school is also developing 'composite' modules 'showing how experiences, knowledge and abilities common to a number of courses may be accredited.[2] Other measures include careful *tutorial guidance* through a series of elective modules, as at Peers School (see page 61); a balancing of the units followed by *timetable blocking* (see Ysgol Emrys ap Iwan, page 143); or a *pre-structuring* of the material (see Buckinghamshire College of Higher Education, page 90). In addition, *record-keeping*

---

[1] Hemsworth High School *A Review of Hemsworth High School Experience in Unit Accreditation*, 1986, pp 6–7

that is diagnostic as well as monitorial is important – as highlighted in Chapter 10.

It is often the case that, although the choice between modules is completely free, they are devised solely by members of staff. Their content, while containing much exciting and imaginative work, may be pre-planned to the extent that it pre-empts any original contribution that pupils are willing or able to make. The emphasis even in the most open of schemes can thus be focused predominantly on what is supplied in terms of curricular input rather than drawing the pupils more closely into the process and giving them a far more active role in negotiating their progress through the module.

For such pupil involvement to take place – and for courses to be as truly related to individual need as many of them claim to be – every battery of units should offer opportunities for those who wish, and are able, to take greater responsibility for their own learning. Such opportunities may enable students to make a piece of work well and truly their own or take part more fully in the running of the module itself. Only when this happens can it be said that we have an *à la carte* curriculum – one that responds to, and develops the talents of all those it was created to serve rather than constraining them.

This chapter is concerned with schemes which attempt just this – chiefly those at the right-hand extremity of the modular transverse. We examine from the inside the way in which, to a greater or lesser extent, they inject a strong element of self-directed and intrinsically motivated learning into their work.

Developmental units

A tentative approach in this direction was seen with *modular banking* (pages 102 and 151), but it can be taken further – although in somewhat less structured a manner – if the teacher prepares the outline for a series of linked (sequential) units and then permits the pupils to develop each, under his guidance, as they see fit. Curricular Item 35 is an example of such an outline.

CURRICULAR ITEM 35
Developmental Units, Aireborough Grammar School, Leeds

The course is structured in such a way as to make it clear to each pupil exactly what is expected of them at any particular time. This

CURRICULAR ITEM 35 (continued)

is done by 'building' each module out of series of weekly task sheets which define in close detail the task in hand in each lesson. The task sheets also outline what the pupil should know at the end of the task, and what they should know how to do. This provides the pupils with short-term goals for achievement.

Great stress is laid on group work and the solution of problems by discussion and debate. Pupils are expected to report back – orally – to the rest of the group on the progress of their work. Practical problems are another feature of the course and this aids the acquisition by pupils of the process skills that are assessed.

TASK SHEET

Each module will be split up into a series of tasks. The task set describes what you will be working on in any particular lesson and the purpose of doing it. It will also set what you should know and what you should know how to do after completing the task.

Module   Business foundation

Task   3

Purpose of task
To decide, on the basis of market research, costings, and sales forecasts, the type and quantity of paper to produce.

Activities
1   Assuming that the results of the questionnaire are to hand, make a decision on the type of paper to produce.
2   Make sketches or 'paste-ups' of possible layouts after checking to see if these are possible.
3   Complete costings based on a certain print run.

What you should have learnt
By the end of this task you should have an understanding of:
1   the role of market research in designing a new product;
2   costings and the relationship between the various types of costs and output;
3   the possibilities of various newspaper layouts working within certain constraints.

What you should have done
As well as understanding the material you should have:

CURRICULAR ITEM 35 (continued)

1   produced your own questionnaire and discussed it with the group;
2   produced and discussed costing statements;
3   discussed the layout of your newspaper, making contributions to group effort.

Reproduced with permission from Aireborough Grammar School, Leeds.

Modular shaping

A third approach gives the pupils even greater responsibility for their own learning. Here, rather than working within the confines of a pre-planned unit, the module is actually shaped in length, design and format according to the different skills, preferences and expertise of those taking part in the scheme. It is based on a team-teaching situation in which a group of staff – drawn in the following case study from the areas of History, Geography and Religious Studies – work closely together within a timetable which has been blocked for this purpose. There is, of course, no reason why it should not be developed within a single Department or Faculty.

CASE STUDY FOURTEEN
Modular Developments within Team Teaching

The approach does not represent groupings for mere convenience, or as an end in itself. Here it is used as a method of harnessing a variety of aptitudes, abilities, and experience for the common good. It takes account of the purpose of mixed-ability teaching and lends itself to some exciting and varied approaches. In essence it is the formation of groups not by ability or haphazardly, but by a careful balancing of the different abilities and personalities concerned. The children, as well as the teacher, must know exactly why they are there – 'Peter is with you because he is good at writing'; 'Angela always gets on well with people, she will do some interviewing for you'; 'I wish I could draw and sketch like Tony – that's why he is here'.

Structuring in success

This kind of approach is far more positive than the others. It begins with something that can be achieved and works outwards from this point. Each child, although working together on some joint project, is really making a unique and individual contribution to the whole. Success in some aspect of the work is the starting-point; co-operation between a series of such 'successes' the basis of such grouping.

If follow-up work is conducted within a form or class, the children can be organized along these lines by the teacher concerned. If, however, it is decided that the whole venture should be run co-operatively the total year group may be so divided, with appropriately sized groups tackling each different aspect of the study. In either case it will be found that the kind of approach here indicated may well bring about radical changes in overall framework and organization.

The theme being studied may be, for example, 'The Middle Ages', and the staff drawn from the history, geography, English, and religious education departments. Following a stimulating lead lesson, open to many different interpretations and dealing with a variety of aspects of life at this time, each class will decide to concentrate on one 'topic' within the whole. One of them may choose 'The Mediaeval village', for example, another 'The Town', a third 'Monasteries', a fourth 'Crusades', class five may select 'Farming', and class six 'Fairs and travel'. Topics should not be duplicated if possible, which may mean that a list of all the topics that can be handled — given the material and staffing available — has to be made. Teachers may make the choice for their class, although it would be more in keeping with the general approach if the children were allowed to do this.

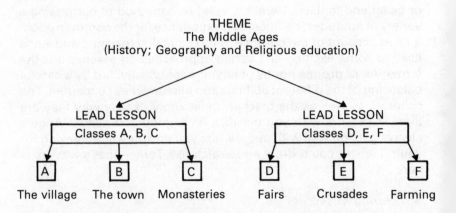

THEME
The Middle Ages
(History; Geography and Religious education)

LEAD LESSON — Classes A, B, C
A — The village
B — The town
C — Monasteries

LEAD LESSON — Classes D, E, F
D — Fairs
E — Crusades
F — Farming

If the scheme is introduced at the beginning of the school year and links have not yet been formed between individual teachers and classes or groups, staff now choose the topics in which they feel most confidence. 'Monasteries' and 'Crusades' would be obvious choices for the R.E. teacher, 'Towns' and 'Villages' for historians, 'Farming' for the geographers. Should such an allocation of staff prove difficult, follow-up work under the direction of any member of the team is made possible by a careful preparation of materials, books, and equipment. This will have to be done well in advance of the project in any case.

Each class will now divide its topic under sub-headings. The topic 'The Mediaeval village', for instance, may be subdivided into 'The manor', 'The land', 'The church', 'Fairs and travel', 'Trades and occupation', 'Costumes and armour'.

It will be seen that here the various subjects in the scheme are all actively involved in its implementation.

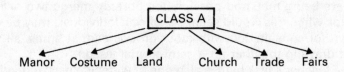

In a class of thirty-six children, groups of six will be allocated as previously described to each sub-topic. Thus, within each small group, a variety of approaches will be adopted. Sketches will be made, accounts written, models constructed, local sources discovered, interviews recorded, drawings completed, drama and mime prepared, research carried out, and so on.

The emerging picture, then, is as follows:

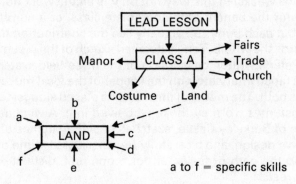

Should the complete year group split on this basis without any previous division into classes, a good deal of previous knowledge about the children will be required. Each member of the team is now responsible for the composition and supervision of several such groupings, and the size of each will largely depend upon the nature of the work undertaken. Whichever approach is decided upon, the teacher's role is as important as that of his colleague within a conventionally organized classroom, but the nature of that role very different.

The role of the teacher

Once a project is underway the teacher acts in an advisory capacity. He knows what material and equipment is available and where various pieces of information can be obtained. Careful planning has ensured this. He also has up-to-date knowledge of what each group is doing and can thus direct discussion or research if difficulties are being met, and possibly temporarily merge two or more groups when this would seem beneficial. Individuals may be withdrawn for consultation with other groups and, at times, all units need drawing together for a semi-formal lesson.

The teacher's task here is also one of widening each individual's horizon. Using initial achievement, which is ensured by careful grouping, each pupil must now be actively encouraged to take a step outside his 'specialization', be it drawing, modelling, writing, research, etc. This may prove difficult at first, but as each child finds that not only is he an active member of a small 'team', but also that the results of his work are actually being incorporated into its findings, the effects are usually extremely gratifying.

A breakthrough here can quite often be engineered by organizing a small classroom exhibition at the end of a set period of time, say four or five weeks. In this way not only is all the work done drawn together for the benefit of the complete class, or a number of the groups, but each pupil can actually see the contribution he is making towards the whole. Tony's detailed sketch of the plough is there next to Peter's written description of the three-field system, whilst Angela's taped interview with the keeper of the local museum complements both. The model of the manor is placed alongside pictures of the costumes worn by those who lived in it. A vivid account of the siege of Berkeley Castle, sketches of siege-engines of the children's own design, and a carefully re-constructed mime on knighthood and the oath of fealty, all form one unit, distinct yet linked with the rest.

When the contribution that the individual has to make is positively emphasized in all these ways, the results are sometimes startling. Not only does the standard of his special 'ability' improve, but quite often his whole attitude and behaviour as well. Having gained self-respect, he can now treat others as individuals to be respected. His work in other fields often slowly progresses, and he can now be persuaded to enhance his model by the addition of short cogent sentences, or paragraphs describing its main features or how it was constructed. The importance of mathematical accuracy can be recognized when it relates to his precise piece of work. More care is taken over labelling and presentation; ideas for improvement are readily forthcoming.

It is one of the joys of this kind of work that it is, to a large extent, self-perpetuating. The children can see it taking shape before them; they have a positive hand in its direction. All are working towards a common goal, and upon the strength and weakness of their combined efforts it will untimately succeed or fail. Responsibility for this is shared by all – pupils and teachers alike.

Reproduced with permission from D. Warwick, *Team Teaching*, Hodder and Stoughton, 1971, pp. 76–79.

Benefits and difficulties

The benefits of this kind of modular work speak for themselves, but the following 'intellectual, social and personal qualities' developed by such an approach have recently been listed following research by the University of Sheffield into *Co-Operative Group Work:*[2]

1   **Skills of communication**
     expressing a point of view
     using visual and verbal means to put ideas across
     developing a sense of audience (communicating in pairs, in small groups, to the whole class, etc)
     developing a vocabulary for different areas of experience (eg, transactional, poetic, expressive modes of communication)
     creating a forum for the exchange of ideas

2   **Skills of learning and understanding**
     learning effectively
     grasping new concepts
     testing tentative hypotheses
     using the group as a resource

---

[2]   Cowie, H *A Study of Teachers' Perceptions of Co-operative Group Work in the Classroom* First report, Co-operative Group Work Project, based at the University of Sheffield Division of Education and funded by British Petroleum Company plc (University of Sheffield, 1986).

> learning to use resources effectively
> interpreting and analysing data
> learning to use primary and secondary sources

3   **Development as a person**
> playing an effective part in the group
> showing initiative
> having confidence in one's own ideas
> having self-respect
> being flexible, trusting, sharing
> becoming sensitive to others
> developing social perspective – taking skills

4   **Skills of co-operation**
> sharing problems
> helping one another
> using the group as a resource
> pooling areas of interest and expertise, exchanging the traditional teacher–pupil relationship
> listening to others
> taking the perspective of others
> coping with silence, non-participation, etc
> developing empathy

The difficulties encountered by the Sheffield teachers were summarised as:

1   *Discipline problems*: loss of control; absenteeism; failure to learn; rejection of method by pupils; group work not perceived as real work by the pupils.

2   *The examination system*: following a syllabus; covering assignments; making sure the pupils know the right answers.

3   *The assessment of the individual within the group*

4   *Physical constraints*: resources, rooms, space.

Student-generated modules

At sixth form level and beyond there is no reason why certain modules in the non-examined part of the curriculum should not actually be led by students themselves. Several of the young men and women in our schools and colleges possess skills which ought to be a credit to the institution. From first-hand experience there comes to mind the young lady about to enter a top professional dance troupe, the English national Under Eighteen football captain, the inventor of a patented piece of kitchen equipment. These, and many others like them, can – with administrative back-up and some tutorial oversight – run successful modules which the staff may not have the expertise to mount.

This is not only an enriching experience for the institution concerned and those who attend the modules; it can also prove beneficial to those actually running the units. There are few surer ways of learning more about a topic than having to teach it – the necessity of isolating concepts, ordering them in an appropriate manner and then getting them across in a simple, direct way can enhance one's own learning every bit as much as it does those at the receiving end.

Independent learning

The opportunity for students to develop their own ideas, either as part of an on-going course or within a scheme of General Studies, is facilitated through modular timetabling. Here, under tutorial supervision, topics may be chosen, research conducted, the project written up and – in some cases – presented as part of a portfolio for external certification. As has been said, it may also be felt that within any group of complementary modules some opportunity should be given for those who cannot find precisely what they want, or who wish to develop ideas of their own. This is particularly the case at Sixth Form level although, if no experience has been gained in the process lower down the school, the results may not be those expected! Such an approach could be facilitated by a school gathering into tutorial groupings all those engaged on work of this kind across the curriculum and placing these groups under teachers especially adept at working in this way.

This is, of course, a high-risk venture no matter how it is planned. Unless carefully thought out, it can all too easily degenerate into pseudo-scholastic time-serving of the worst kind. On the surface, all might appear to be earnest and high-minded but, in reality, an academic charade could well be in progress – one in which the uninitiated pursue the unobtainable down labyrinthine corridors neither illuminated by a spark of ingenuity nor warmed by a glow of enthusiasm.

If this is to be avoided, independent learning needs to be well planned and carefully monitored. In no way does it entail an abrogation of a teacher's professional function. Students will be working much of the time by themselves and will use far more personal initiative than might otherwise be required. But in order for their work to have shape and purpose, they will need help and possibly direction, especially in the important early stages. Encouragement and sympathetic understanding will also be required. Tutorial skills of a high order (to be explored more fully in the final chapter) are the pre-requisites for staffing such enterprises, as well as a large range of information and up-to-date knowledge of all local sources that may be tapped.

Establishing the group

The first stage in setting up such a programme is to ensure that all those entering it have the personal motivation to work independently under the minimum of extrinsic control or, better still, have a potential that self-directed learning will help to develop. There is something to be said for individuals 'earning' the right to work in this way; certainly they will be under probation in its early stages. It is a case of each working to his capability, not competitively, and does not necessarily involve obtaining outstanding results. It would, after all, be fatal for the success of the scheme were disciplinary problems to arise or if it became a 'soft option' – either for students or the staff involved!

Students will be working mainly by themselves, but most modular approaches place them in groups with others undertaking similar research and responsibile to the same tutor. Sessions will be timetabled in which the group come together and discuss items of common interest arising from their work. Other sessions may be spent in individual tuition and in this case the other students in the group may well be in different parts of the building or locality, furthering or writing up their research. Between tutorials, individual sessions may be requested by any member of the group.

The work undertaken by individuals could relate to one of their main subject areas (possibly at 'A' level or within TVEI or CPVE schemes) and hence these sessions can be regarded as complementary modules. It is not, however, recommended that the whole group tackle the same project. This could hardly be interpreted as 'independent learning'!

Group sessions will probably be timetabled for one period each week and last for a single or double lesson. Each group should not really consist of more than eight individuals, or the load on the tutor will become too great and, for the student, the process could become too diffuse. From the very outset the all-important tutorial relationship needs to be made apparent. The teacher is here once more operating in an advisory capacity – as a facilitator of learning, and one who is extremely interested in the successful outcome of each project. And here it should be made clear – 'successful outcome' is not a pedagogic laying-on-of-hands, in which every conceivable book on the topic is accumulated and large sections from each are transcribed. Rather, it entails reading carefully round a subject, picking up central ideas or concepts, arriving at some sort of a *gestalt* or overview and then following this through in as individual a way as possible. All this may sound beyond most of our students. The tragedy is that so few of them are allowed to operate in this way and, if they are, such little support of the right kind is given to them.

Laying the groundwork

A structured scheme of study-skills could run throughout a school, or modules of this kind may be developed within departments. In either case, the task of the tutor will be much easier than it might otherwise have been. Great care still needs to be taken, though, in the early stages of the modules here under review. If the scheme goes wrong at this point, there is little that can save it at a later date. Most students will be eager to choose a topic and to get on with the work immediately; this is commendable in itself but can prove counter-productive if too hasty a decision over content and direction is made. Others in the group will have the intrinsic motivation, but may be unsure as to how to start.

Possibly, then, some time could be spent outlining the different kinds of approach that might be adopted. Time will be saved in the long-run if the kind of resources that might be used are described together with their whereabouts. These resources will not only be found in the school, but within the locality – the county library, the information office, the local newspaper and so on. Nor should human resources be forgotten. Chief among these will be members of staff, both in their professional capacity and as the possessors of useful funds of first-hand information relating to their hobbies, interests and out-of-school activities.

It is extremely helpful if the group can make an initial visit to local resource centres together with their tutor. They can then be taken round, meet the person in charge and perhaps be given a brief introductory talk. Future visits will not then be made 'cold' and the foundations of a good working relationship may be laid.

An introduction along these lines will not only provide individual students with a range of information from which to start their work, it will also help to bring them together as a group. The tutor needs as far as possible to start from where the students are, allowing information to emerge as a result of questions or follow-up discussion relating to the various outside visits. This will also set the tone of how the group is to operate when they come together in timetabled periods.

Choosing a topic

Individuals may arrive knowing exactly what topic they wish to follow, or with a specific project in mind relating to one of the subjects they are following. In this case, some consultation needs to take place between the Department concerned and the tutor. In fact, if a school wishes to develop this method of approach to any extent, the co-ordinator of such schemes really needs to attend Heads of Subject meetings.

Students unsure as to what topic to follow will require individual sessions with the tutor in which their general background, interests, academic strengths and weaknesses, etc are openly discussed. Some tutors provide lists of possible topics, or arrange for these to be made available by the department(s) concerned. A complete range of topic sheets could be given to the student to facilitate his choice. Such sheets need to be far more than a bland list of topics, and the tutor responsible for Independent Learning might assist in their preparation so that teachers across a wide range of subjects will become familiar with the way in which he works. The topic should be supported by a brief outline, or synopsis, setting out why it is important to the individual, how he intends following it through and what resources he expects to use. This is important, as it can be most frustrating for someone to set out on a project full of confidence, only to find that either he has not got the background knowledge to sustain it or that the requisite resources to bring it to a successful completion are just not available. A brief pro-forma like that in Figure 8.1 can help to clarify the student's ideas and form a basis for early discussion with the tutor.

Developing the work

The balance referred to earlier, between individual advice and the sharing of common problems, continues as the different projects take shape. The weekly timetabled sessions will provide the main focus for both elements. During these periods, support and guidance can be given to individuals while more general discussion can take place over problems that have

---

Figure 8.1

NAME ....   DATE ....

TITLE OF TOPIC ....

SUBJECT AREA(S) ....

EXAMINATION ....   COMPLETION DATE ....

BRIEF OUTLINE ....

....

RESOURCES REQUIRED ....

---

been encountered. There will be an open sharing of information and common themes should emerge relating to methodology and perhaps even to content. Members of the group can learn much from one another through such exchanges, with an added bonus if they come from contrasting areas of the curriculum. The empirical scientific approach can, for example, spark off some lively exchanges if contrasted with the more deductive literary one; the way a mathematician tackles a problem could provide additional insights, and so on.

As far as the individual student is concerned, the tutor should check, through an adequate record-keeping system, that progress is maintained. Once more, it is not so much a question of telling him what should be done next – the project is, after all, his own – as of entering into discussion over what steps need to be taken and what should follow. A series of targets is often negotiated; these, although flexible enough to be modified, brought forward or delayed, nevertheless form a syllabus for the unit. At the conclusion of each session, the tutor could outline the outcome of the discussion in a few sentences on one page of a small duplicate receipt book. The student signs this and takes away the top copy; the tutor retains the bottom one as the basis for their next meeting. A series of such brief comments forms a useful commentary on progress and may provide the basis for a profile, if required.

Completing the project

The tutor will have seen all the projects emerge, section by section, in draft form and – hopefully – members of the group will share in one another's successes and assist over difficulties. The department or departments most related to each piece of work will also have been involved from the outset. As each project reaches its conclusion, advice of a more general nature should be forthcoming, from the Art Department, for example, on the use of illustrations, the Mathematics Department on the use of graphs in survey findings, Geography on maps, English on style, Modern Languages on translation, etc. The culmination of the process is reached when each student makes a presentation, in one form or another, to the rest of the group.

Just how much further the projects should go is a matter of some contention. Should work of this kind be formally assessed? Need there be any evaluation of the outcome other than a suitably worded Modular Credit? If external examinations are concerned this must, of course, be the case, but many teachers believe that such work is an end in itself. This being the case, no assessment other than regular monitoring of the scheme by the tutor is required. To go further, it is said, would be to place the wrong emphasis on the project from the start, leading to competition rather than co-operation and focusing attention on the way the work was presented rather than its individual content.

Against this, it is argued that evaluation has been taking place throughout the project. To try to hide any summative assessment, therefore, is dishonest to all concerned, does nothing to encourage those who have taken trouble over their work, and devalues the idea of unitary credits.

The benefits of choice

There is a strong element of choice within most modular schemes, especially the ones featured in this chapter. Where this is less accentuated, the sharing of objectives between teacher and taught remains. Both of these are strongly motivating factors in their own right, but behind them lie a range of larger issues related to the society which the school serves and the nature of the world in which our pupils will be living out the rest of their days. Today, perhaps more than ever before, there are those on hand to help the disadvantaged, and, of course, information is available for the taking if it is required. But if the individual does not know where to look or who to ask; is unable to frame his queries in an understandable fashion; lacks the minimal technical competence needed to key them in; if he is, indeed, incapable of interpreting the answers once he gets them . . . his future will be bleak.

We seem to be creating a self-service society where flexibility of mind and outlook are of cardinal importance. The industries and technologies developing today call for initiative, personal responsibility and an enquiring mind. In the world of tomorrow the 'scientific' values of research and discovery will rate more highly than the passive virtues of know-how and information. Moreover, at a time of increased leisure, greater self-sufficiency is going to be needed. Enquiry, research, a critical mind and sound judgement – all these qualities will be at a premium.

In the late 1980s and early '90s, an individual could well be disadvantaged or penalised if he has received too narrow, too formal or too dependency-based a schooling. Hence the wider values implicit in all or the more open modular schemes. The hidden curriculum operates as clearly here as it does elsewhere, as Case Study Fifteen illustrates.

CASE STUDY FIFTEEN
The Hidden Curriculum in Modular Planning

A project in one of the younger nations took as its key theme *Political Self-Determination* and a modular scheme was implemented. The teachers busied themselves preparing their materials. These included extracts from the speeches of the great leaders who had helped throw off the imperial yoke, film of new social developments, lessons on the aims of the new society, lectures on the role of the individual within it, and an impressive list of visiting speakers.

The pupils were given plenty to do. They were to write essays, listen to the talks, take part in well-organised debates, watch videos, take notes from lessons, give short lecturettes from pre-specified lists, and so on.

Each module was extremely well planned and brilliantly executed. The teaching was of a high calibre and the lectures inspiring in the extreme. The pupils were well motivated and, on the face of it, the scheme had been a great success.

But beneath all this lay a hidden curriculum, pointing the pupils in a direction quite opposite to that contained within the programme's aims. These, it will be remembered, were to do with *Political Self-Determination*. Yet, nowhere in the course were the participants given even a modicum of choice, decision-making within the scheme as a whole was non-existent. As an exercise in national history and civics, it was impressive, but the real lessons being learnt were light years away from the setting of one's own goals in life. They related, it seemed, far more to listening patiently to what you were told, doing what you were instructed to do, and feeling grateful for what you were given.

For further reading

The development of the kind of work traced in this chapter at primary level is treated by P Cunningham in *Tradition and Innovation: Progressivism in Primary Education since 1944* (Falmer, 1987), while the longitudinal development of the work is considered in Norman Beswick's *Re-thinking Active Learning, 8–16* (Falmer 1987). At secondary level, L Button's *Developing Group Work with Adolescents* (Hodder and Stoughton, 1979), N N Collins' *New Teaching Skills* (Oxford University Press, 1986) and the FEU's *Flexible Learning Opportunities* (1983) are all useful. The importance of analysing such work as it proceeds is dealt with by D Hopkins in *A Teacher's Guide to Classroom Research* (Open University, 1985), by H D Cassidy and T Cuff in *Action Research in Classrooms and Schools* (Basil Blackwell, 1984) and by P Croll in *Systematic Classroom Observation* (Falmer, 1986).

9 Records of Progress

Record keeping within any curricular area serves two broad purposes – that of monitoring progress through a set programme of work, and that of indicating the future steps that need to be taken. Like the Roman god Janus, it looks in both directions, each of which has implications for modular planning.

Monitoring modular schemes

Within more formal approaches the monitorial function will take precedence. Here each individual's progress through the units of work can be checked by reference to essay grades, test scores, homework marks, contribution to classroom discussion, practical skills, and so on. These may be entered on to a register of the conventional kind, sub-divided laterally into divisions which correspond to the sequence of units.

If an element of choice enters into such schemes, with individuals in a class or throughout the department opting for certain alternative sections of the syllabus, then previous records of achievement will take on an added significance. These will be contributory factors in the selection of the most appropriate material and need to be readily available to all those involved in the decision-making process: pupils, teachers and the tutorial staff.

When a completely free choice is to be made, then such records will be doubly important. For the pupil they will provide a basis for the construction of a personal curriculum which is at once dynamic, balanced and coherent; for the parents, evidence of progress through schemes which can appear baffling in their complexity; for the school, an excellent way of building overall aims directly into each individual programme of work.

Such elements are often brought together within the unit credits issued at the completion of each module. An extremely useful example is that taken from the Thomas Tallis School, reproduced in Curricular Item 36.

CURRICULAR ITEM 36
Draft Modular Credit, Thomas Tallis School, London

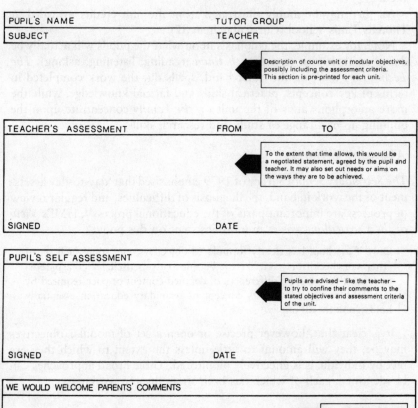

Thomas Tallis School

CREDIT

PUPIL'S NAME	TUTOR GROUP
SUBJECT	TEACHER

> Description of course unit or modular objectives, possibly including the assessment criteria. This section is pre-printed for each unit.

TEACHER'S ASSESSMENT	FROM	TO

> To the extent that time allows, this would be a negotiated statement, agreed by the pupil and teacher. It may also set out needs or aims on the ways they are to be achieved.

SIGNED   DATE

PUPIL'S SELF ASSESSMENT

> Pupils are advised – like the teacher – to try to confine their comments to the stated objectives and assessment criteria of the unit.

SIGNED   DATE

WE WOULD WELCOME PARENTS' COMMENTS

> The pupil's achievements in terms of the above learning objectives and assessment criteria.

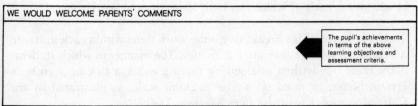

Reproduced by permission of Thomas Tallis School.

Making use of objectives

The importance of stating objectives unambiguously in terms of what will actually be done within each module, together with an explicit statement regarding content, should now be apparent. This facilitates choice not only by making it abundantly clear just what is available, but also by providing a track record regarding what has already been achieved. Record keeping and planning through objectives are thus clearly interrelated.

All this may be amply illustrated from the unit credits awarded at Thomas Tallis School (Curricular Item 37).

Note, for example, the emphasis upon what the pupils will actually be doing on their visit to a *French town* (reading; listening; asking). *The Technology unit*, on the other hand, spells out the work completed in terms of key concepts, practical skills and factual knowledge, while the more amorphous aims of the unit on *the Family* concentrate upon the building up of a range of study and research skills.

Assessing progress

The Secondary School Survey of 1979 emphasised that 'day-to-day assessment of the work in hand, the diagnosis of difficulties, and regular review of progress are important parts of the educational process'[1]. HMI's *View of the Curriculum* was even more insistent on this point:

> Only if a school has clearly formulated objectives, and some such set of criteria or checklist . . . is it likely to be able to assure itself, let alone parents or others, that despite differences of detailed content or pace required by pupils' differing abilities, its concept of secondary education essentially holds good for all pupils.[2]

It is clear that, however precise or open a set of modular objectives may be, they will amount to little unless the extent to which they are met by individuals is effectively monitored. Three broad approaches can be identified, each of which has both strengths and weaknesses:

1 *Merit Rating* This breaks down the work done within each unit into a number of small, behavioural activities. The manner in which students carry these out is then assessed by placing either a tick or a cross in certain boxes, or rated on a five/ten point scale, as illustrated by the Catford School (Curricular Item 38, page 184).

Such an approach has the great merit of ensuring that all the skills relating to any area have been considered and of enabling pupils to see

---

[1]   HMI *Aspects of Secondary Education*. HMSO, 1979, p.263.
[2]   HMI *A View of the Curriculum*. HMSO, 1980, p.15.

CURRICULAR ITEM 37
Modular Credits, Thomas Tallis School, London

PUPIL'S NAME	TUTOR GROUP
SUBJECT TECHNOLOGY	TEACHER

This pupil has completed the Computer Control and Micro-Electronics unit of the technology course.

Key concepts: Circuit building and design; computer programming; computer control of digital/analogue input and output devices; robot design; safety.

Practical skills: 'hands-on' computing/programming experience; circuit building and design; problem-solving; interaction between computers and suitable peripheral devices.

Factual knowledge: computer systems and architecture; interfacing and control; electronic components; logic gates and their uses; Pascal and Basic programming; robotics in industry; analogue and digital devices.

TEACHER'S ASSESSMENT	FROM	TO

A record describing the teacher's assessment is shown overleaf.

SIGNED   DATE

PUPIL'S SELF ASSESSMENT

SIGNED   DATE

WE WOULD WELCOME PARENTS' COMMENTS

CURRICULAR ITEM 37 (continued)

PUPIL'S NAME	TUTOR GROUP
SUBJECT OUTLOOK '87 – THE FAMILY	TEACHER

AIMS: 1 To develop in pupils an understanding of the family & divorce.
2 To foster the skills of essay and article writing.
3 To develop in pupils the ability to marshal an argument.
4 To develop decision-making skills based on information.
5 To develop the ability to generalise from a range of cases.
6 To give information on various types of contraceptives.

TEACHER'S ASSESSMENT	FROM	TO

ASSESSMENT OF THIS UNIT IS AS FOLLOWS:

A An essay on the family. (1,2,3,5)
B Prepare an article. (2,3,5)
C Ability to decide on appropriate contraceptives
   for various circumstances. (4,6).

SIGNED   **DATE**

PUPIL'S SELF ASSESSMENT

SIGNED   **DATE**

WE WOULD WELCOME PARENTS' COMMENTS

CURRICULAR ITEM 37 (continued)

PUPIL'S NAME	TUTOR GROUP
SUBJECT FRENCH CSE	**TEACHER**

Unit: EN VILLE (Around the town)

This unit of work aims to teach pupils to find their way around in a French town.

This involves:

a) Reading street-maps, brochures, street signs and outdoor notices
b) Listening to information and guidance
c) Asking for information and guidance

The pupil's ability to cope in such situations is tested and the results are recorded below.

TEACHER'S ASSESSMENT	FROM	TO
Test Results		
Reading /30		
Listening /40		
Speaking /10		
(Writing /10)		
SIGNED	**DATE**	

PUPIL'S SELF ASSESSMENT
DATE

WE WOULD WELCOME PARENTS' COMMENTS

Reproduced by permission of Thomas Tallis School.

CURRICULAR ITEM 38
Merit Rating, Catford School, London.

UNDERSTANDING

Good Average Poor

- Describe the percentage composition of air.

- Describe an experiment to show that air contains approximately 1/5th oxygen.

- Describe the industrial preparation of oxygen and nitrogen.

- Describe the properties of oxygen.

- Relate the properties of oxygen to its uses.

- Classify oxides as metallic or non metallic. Use the terms 'oxidation' and 'reduction'.

- Draw a fire triangle.

- Use the fire triangle to discuss the best ways of putting fires out.

- Explain how carbon monoxide is produced during combustion.

- Identify the gases causing air pollution.

- Discuss the results of air pollution.

- Describe the circulation of nitrogen in nature.

- Describe the preparation of ammonia in the laboratory.

- Describe the properties of ammonia.

- Carry out and report on tests for ammonia and the ammonium ion.

- Describe how ammonia is converted into fertilizers.

at a glance where their strong points lie. It is also a relatively speedy method of assessment. However, by itself it does not give any indication of how the work was carried out, it could lead to the trivialisation of any endeavour through an endless listing of tiny components, and the very speed with which it can be conducted could lead to abuse. The sum must always be more than the totality of its parts.

2 *Criteria Listing* A series of statements is provided, relating to the kind of activity which typifies performance at various stages in the under-standing of a piece of work, or the performance of a set of skills. This usually takes the form of a grid which can be ticked, blocked in or coloured as the student develops in awareness or competence. The grid associated with the Technology unit on page 181 is shown in Curricular Item 39.

The strength of criteria listing lies in its identification of specific activities; it is far more behavioural in outcome than merit rating, but could have the disadvantage of concentrating too heavily on contributory activities at the expense of the course as a whole. There is also the problem of identifying just when students have reached each stage and the possi-bility that, having attained a certain level, they may remain there for the rest of the course.

3 *Written Comments* Quite wisely, most schools adopting either of the above approaches supplement it with comments of a more substantial nature by those responsible for the course and, in some cases, by the pupils themselves. This is certainly the case in the Catford scheme illus-trated above.

It is obvious that far more is involved in any course than merely an aggregate of its parts. No more can justice be done to skills, abilities, competencies or behaviours on an A–E, or even a 1–1000 grade, however sophisticated the approach. Some schemes therefore substitute spaces for teachers' (and/or pupils') own comments within the matrices, others leave sections blank for broader comments. The major criticism of this approach is its subjectivity and a tendency to generate generalised comments.

Another kind of written comment comes from the students, in the form of either a diary or log book detailing the progress of their work on a weekly basis. If a specific element, such as work experience or a field trip, needs to be monitored, this may be done on a daily basis.

Note also the accumulation of tutor's comments suggested for modules of self-directed learning on page 175.

External examinations

Effective monitoring of the work is especially important if the modular credit to be issued is part of a larger overall examination or if a number

CURRICULAR ITEM 39
Criteria Listing, Thomas Tallis School, London

	Level 1	Level 2	Level 3	Level 4
TALKING AND LISTENING	Can make sensible replies when spoken to	Can hold conversation and can take messages	Can follow and give simple descriptions and explanations	Can communicate effectively with a range of people in variety of situations
WORKING IN A GROUP	Can co-operate with others when asked	Can work with other members of the group to achieve common aims	Can understand own position and results of own actions within the group	Can be active and decisive member of a group
ACCEPTING RESPONSIBILITY	Can follow instructions for simple tasks and carry them out under guidance	Can follow instructions for simple tasks and carry them out independently	Can follow a series of instructions and carry them out independently	Can perform a variety of tasks effectively given minimal guidance
SAFETY	Can explain the need for safety rules	Can remember safety instructions	Can spot safety hazards	Can apply safe working practices independently
USING EQUIPMENT	Can use equipment safely to perform simple tasks under guidance	Can use equipment safely to perform a sequence of tasks after demonstration	Can select and use suitable equipment and materials for the job without help	Can set up and use equipment to produce work to a standard
OBTAINING INFORMATION	Can ask for needed information	Can find needed information with guidance	Can use standard sources of information	Can extract and assemble information from several given sources
ASSESSING OWN RESULTS	Can receive advice about own performance	Can seek advice about own performance	Can assess own results with guidance	Can assess own results for familiar tasks without help
ELECTRONIC COMPONENTS AND CIRCUIT DIAGRAMS	Can recognise electronic components on a circuit diagram	Can solder components onto veroboard as indicated by circuit diagram	Has understood what tasks the various components perform	Has detailed knowledge of individual components and their use
COMPUTER PROGRAMMING	Can effectively use a pre-written program and give correct inputs	Can effectively assess the output from a given program	Can change an existing program to perform a given task	Can unite owns programs to control devices external to computer
COMPUTER CONTROL	Can specify a range of devices that can be controlled by computer	Understands the need for an interface/user part to communicate with external devices	Understands the structure and pin positions of a given microcomputer user part	Can effectively connect and control a device of their own via the user part
STRUCTURE OF THE MICROCOMPUTER	Can recognise the basic units of a computer system	Can correctly set up and operate a computer system	Can load and run a piece of software on a computer system	Understands the relevance and workings of the 3 main elements of the CPU
	Has understood the wide	Has understood what com-	Has understood current trends in computer tech-	Has understood the implications of the use of computers

Reproduced by permission of Thomas Tallis School

of such units go to make up an external award, such as GCSE. Matters of coherence of content and equivalence between individual units need here to be monitored with great precision, and this tends to be easier in subjects where a large degree of empirical evidence is available. Whatever the discipline, however, the emphasis upon behavioural objectives which is closely linked to the modular curriculum, and which coincides with GCSE's stress on criteria-referencing, focuses the teacher's mind on to what his pupils 'know, understand and can do'. From this positive basis considerations of a more aesthetic or subjective nature can be developed.

If the scheme involves modules of a complementary nature and the approach is an open one, then the emphasis will be on ensuring that the course submission covers all the salient points relating to its content and approach, as well as stating precisely how the key elements in each module will be assessed. Guidelines on the submission of Modular Schemes from the Northern Partnership for Records of Achievement were given on page 127. Curricular Item 40 page 188 shows how one school has successfully responded to them.

From this submission it may be noted that an emphasis on precise outcomes may be advantageous in initiating much useful discussion and an increased understanding of the subjective issues involved.

In cases such as this, a moderator will probably be attached to the school to ensure that the submission is adhered to, and adequate staff training will be made available for the newer methodology. Course work will feature largely, as will group activity. So it is important to be absolutely clear as to the exact nature of the evidence that is acceptable. The Northern Partnership for Records of Achievement issue rules and guidelines on acceptable evidence (see Curricular Item 41).

In GCSE units are normally assessed along more formal lines, either internally by the school or externally by the board, if this seems more appropriate. Here, again, it is important to spell out exactly what is required (see Curricular Item 42). Such criteria may then form the basis of a record-card for internal, but moderated use, as shown in Curricular Item 43, and finally appear on grade sheets (Curricular Item 44).

Course coherence

The coherence of schemes which are to be externally examined through modular units is something upon which all the boards quite rightly insist. Each requires prior evidence of this coherence, and may either suggest set patterns which may be followed, or invite schools to submit the 'modular pathway'[3] to be taken.

---

3   Southern Examining Group *The Modular Curriculum, a Discussion Document*, 1986, p.3.

CURRICULAR ITEM 40
Submission of Module for External Accreditation

UNIT ACCREDITATION   **CODE:** NEA/UA/LS/152
SUBMISSION UNIT PROFORMA   **DATE:** 23.6.86

SCHOOL: MIDDLETON PARK HIGH **LEA:** Leeds

UNIT TITLE: Apartheid in South Africa

CURRICULAR AREA: Humanities   **NOTIONAL TIME:** 12hrs.

UNIT DESCRIPTION

This unit is designed to give the student an insight into the working of apartheid in South Africa, by critically examining a variety of historical and contemporary sources.

OUTCOMES TO BE ACCREDITED   **EVIDENCE TO BE OFFERED**

In successfully completing this unit the student will have:

Student's notes (1–5)

• demonstrated the ability to

Teacher's checklist (6)

1 identify differences between the lives of blacks and whites in South Africa, eg mortality, standard of living;
2 identify and compare two strategies for peace in South Africa;

• shown knowledge of
3 a 'typical' life of a young black person in South Africa today;
4 the lifestyles of black and white people in South Africa;
5 the life and work of one black leader;

• experienced
6 a group discussion on apartheid and its treatment by the media.

PROCEDURES FOR MAKING AND RECORDING ASSESSMENT

Teachers will record, date and sign each completed piece of work offered as evidence of the outcomes.

CURRICULAR ITEM 41
Admissible Evidence

**THE SPECIFYING OF EVIDENCE OF ACHIEVEMENT
IN THE UNIT SUBMISSION**

Evidence for the successful completion of a unit

a   When submitting units for validation, centres are required to specify the intended learning outcomes of the unit and to indicate for each outcome what evidence of each student's achievement of the outcome will be retained by the centre and made available to the NEA assessor.

b   During the first year of operation of the interim scheme certain difficulties have been encountered, first by centres in specifying appropriate evidence for some kinds of outcomes, particuarly those relating to a student's experience of a process, and, second, by assessors in confirming that the evidence which they inspected did in practice confirm the achievement of an outcome.

c   It is accepted that these difficulties do not arise specifically from the interim scheme and that they would be encountered in any system which sought to confirm any achievement which, for example, has no tangible product or which results from a group activity. Nevertheless, it is evident that some centres are not paying sufficient attention, on occasions, to the suitability of the evidence to be offered and in particular that undue reliance is being placed on the use of checklists or records, sometimes in circumstances in which more direct evidence of achievement is available.

Evidence of a student's achievements can be grouped under a number of headings

a   Primary evidence in the form of, for example, a piece of written or graphical work or a finished product.

b   Primary evidence in the form of, for example, a tape or video recording or a photograph.

c   Secondary evidence in the form of a record, completed by the teacher, the student or the teacher and the student.

CURRICULAR ITEM 41 (continued)

d   Secondary evidence in the form of a checklist compiled by a teacher.

So long as the evidence of achievement is properly gathered and presented each of the four types can be equally valid and acceptable, and the nature of the individual learning outcomes will determine which type of evidence is most appropriate.

The following guidelines should be followed by centres in specifying evidence in a unit submission

a   Where primary evidence of an outcome can be made available it should always be included.

b   It is not acceptable for the ONLY evidence of achievement for an entire unit to consist of a checklist compiled by a teacher, which merely indicates the successful achievement of each outcome by means of a tick, whether signed and dated or not.

Evidence for the contribution of individual students to group activities

a   Many units which have been validated have elements of group activity within them and a student's ability to work as a member of a group is increasingly being seen by centres as an essential skill to be acquired.

b   Group activities can be categorised under two headings.
   i   Activities in which the focus of assessment is the interaction of one student with another (e.g. drama, discussion) and which, therefore, can only be carried out within a group.
   ii Activities in which students work together on a task which could be completed by a single student but which is carried out jointly because it would either take too long or demand excessive resources for each student to work alone.

In either case it would normally be possible for primary evidence of the group's achievements to be retained. Difficulties have arisen, however, in the identification of the contribution of the individual to the group.

CURRICULAR ITEM 41 (continued)

c Three strategies have been developed by LEAs for acknowledging the contribution of individual students to a group activity.

  i A checklist for skills demonstrated during group work, an example of which is included in Appendix 2, *Assessing the individual student's contribution to a group task.*

  ii A log or diary, maintained by the student, recording the student's contribution to the work of the group, or, a printed record on which student and teacher confirm stages of progression in an activity by commenting, signing and dating.

  iii The specifying of outcomes relating to group work in terms such as
  'To participate as a member of a group in the production of ... '
  rather than
  'To produce ... '.

The use of checklists and records as evidence

a During the first year of the operation of the scheme difficulties have arisen from the extensive use of checklists and records as evidence, especially in units where primary evidence of achievement could have been made available and also in circumstances in which the unit submission made reference to a record or checklist without indicating its nature or its contents.

b There are very few units in which a checklist will be accepted as the only evidence of achievement. In the rare circumstances where a checklist alone would provide the most appropriate form of evidence, it is essential that it break down any generalised outcomes into detailed subskills.

c Any checklist (or record with a printed format) to be offered as evidence must be attached to the unit submission so that the LEA pre-validating committee and regional validating committee may consider its suitability for its purpose. Such a unit will not be considered for validation in the absence of the checklist or printed record.

The use of formal tests as evidence

It is unlikely that a test will confirm the successful achievement of a single outcome; it is more likely that it will relate to a number

CURRICULAR ITEM 41 (continued)

of outcomes. In these circumstances it is important that the student should be given the opportunity to demonstrate in the test that each individual outcome has been achieved. It must be emphasised that a high overall mark on a test cannot be seen as compensating for a failure to achieve a specific outcome.

The use of copied material as evidence

a   During the first year of operation of the scheme concern has been expressed by assessors that the evidence of achievement presented by some centres for some units shows signs of extensive copying by all students from a common source. Such copying falls into two categories.

i   Work copied from text books or similar sources.

ii   Work copied from a blackboard at the instigation of the teacher, deriving perhaps from group work in class, and used as evidence of an individual student's achievement.

b   i   Appropriate copying from text books etc. is permitted so long as the extent of the copying and the source are properly and clearly acknowledged at an appropriate point in the work of each student.

ii   The achievement of an outcome can only be confirmed by appropriate evidence of individual pupil work, unless a reference to group work is made in the specification of the outcome in the unit submission.

Reproduced by permission from *Unit Accreditation (Interim Scheme), Rules and Guidelines*, Northern Partnership for Records of Achievement, pp.11–13.

CURRICULAR ITEM 42
Criteria for Modular Science

4.   GROUPING AND WEIGHTING OF ASSESSMENT OBJECTIVES

4.1 For the purpose of making assessments, the assessment objectives have been grouped and weighted as shown in the table below. The assessment objectives included within each group, and their relationship with the aims, are indicated by the reference numbers.

CURRICULAR ITEM 42 (continued)

	Weightings	Assessment Objectives	Aims
KNOWLEDGE, UNDERSTANDING		3.1.1	2.1.1
AND APPLICATION		3.1.2	2.1.2
		3.1.3	2.1.3
4.1.1 Knowledge	10–15%)	3.1.4	2.2.1
	)	3.1.5	2.2.2
4.1.2 Understanding	15–25%) 45%	3.2.3	2.2.3
	)	3.2.11	2.3.1
4.1.3 Application	10–15%)	3.2.12	2.3.2
		3.2.13	2.4.1
		3.2.16	2.4.2
PRACTICAL AND EXPERIMENTAL			
SKILLS			
4.1.4 Select and use			
apparatus	5%)	3.1.3	2.1.1
	)	3.2.1	2.1.2
4.1.5 Make accurate	)	3.2.2	2.1.3
observations	5%)	3.2.3	2.2.1
	)	3.2.6	2.2.2
4.1.6 Interpret and draw	)	3.2.7	2.2.3
conclusions	5%)	3.2.8	2.3.1
	) 30%	3.2.9	2.3.2
4.1.7 Communicate about	)	3.2.10	2.4.1
experiments	5%)	3.2.13	
	)		
4.1.8 Devise and organise	)		
experiments	5%)		
	)		
4.1.9 Solve technological	)		
problems	5%)		
INFORMATION HANDLING,			
INTERPRETATION AND EVALUATION			
4.1.10 Information handling	)	3.2.3	2.1.1
	)	3.2.4	2.1.2
4.1.11 Interpretation	) 25%*	3.2.5	2.1.3
	)	3.2.6	2.2.1
4.1.12 Evaluation	)	3.2.7	2.2.2
		3.2.9	
		3.2.12	
		3.2.13	
		3.2.14	
		3.2.15	
		3.2.16	

*Allocated to skills and abilities in approximately equal proportions.

Reproduced with permission from *Modular Science*, Northern Partnership for Records of Achievement 1986, p.11.

CURRICULAR ITEM 43
Recording Criteria

NORTHERN EXAMINING ASSOCIATION

INDIVIDUAL RECORD CARD

MODULAR SCIENCE SCHEME A

SECOND AWARD

ASSESSMENT SET

PRACTICAL AND EXPERIMENTAL SKILLS

Teacher	Date	Assignment reference	MARKS FOR SKILLS (Each assessed on FOUR occasions)					
			Select and use apparatus	Make accurate observations	Interpret data and draw conclusions	Communicate about experiments	Devise and organise experiments	Solving technological problems
TOTALS			/16	/16	/16	/16	/16	/16

OVERALL TOTAL [   ] × 0.36 [   ]

MODULE TESTS

Teacher	Date		Title of Module	Mark/40
		·1		
		2		
		3		
		4		
		5		
		6		
		7		
			TOTAL	× 0.16

Title for certification [CORE and   ]

This is to certify that the marks shown on this record card were awarded in accordance with the *Instructions and guidance for teachers* and that every reasonable step has been taken to ensure that the assessment is based on the individual work of the candidate concerned.

Signature(s) of teacher(s) responsible for the assessment

This record card is to be retained until after the publication of results. It is to be made available on request to a moderator.

Reproduced with permission from *Modular Science*, Northern Partnership for Records of Achievement, 1986.

CURRICULAR ITEM 44
Record Card

CANDIDATE RECORD CARD　　　　　　　　　　　　　　　　　　**SCHEME B**
(for Coursework Assessment and Module Tests)　　SINGLE/FIRST AWARD (use reverse also for Double Award)

CENTRE NAME	CANDIDATE NAME	ASSESSMENT SET
CENTRE NUMBER	CANDIDATE NUMBER	

MODULE TITLE _____

Assessment Objective	A	B	C	D	E	F	
Raw Score (Max 10)							
Weight Factor	x1	x1	x1	x2	x2	x3	Total
Scaled Score	10	10	10	20	20	30	100

Module Test 40

MODULE TITLE _____

Assessment Objective	A	B	C	D	E	F	
Raw Score (Max 10)							
Weight Factor	x1	x1	x1	x2	x2	x3	Total
Scaled Score	10	10	10	20	20	30	100

Module Test 40

MODULE TITLE _____

Assessment Objective	A	B	C	D	E	F	
Raw Score (Max 10)							
Weight Factor	x1	x1	x1	x2	x2	x3	Total
Scaled Score	10	10	10	20	20	30	100

Module Test 40

MODULE TITLE _____

Assessment Objective	A	B	C	D	E	F	
Raw Score (Max 10)							
Weight Factor	x1	x1	x1	x2	x2	x3	Total
Scaled Score	10	10	10	20	20	30	100

Module Test 40

MODULE TITLE _____

Assessment Objective	A	B	C	D	E	F	
Raw Score (Max 10)							
Weight Factor	x1	x1	x1	x2	x2	x3	Total
Scaled Score	10	10	10	20	20	30	100

Module Test 40

MODULE TITLE _____

Assessment Objective	A	B	C	D	E	F	
Raw Score (Max 10)							
Weight Factor	x1	x1	x1	x2	x2	x3	Total
Scaled Score	10	10	10	20	20	30	100

Module Test 40

Title for Certification	+

This is to certify that the marks shown on this record card were awarded in accordance with the *Instructions and guidance for teachers* and that every reasonable step has been taken to ensure that the assessment is based on the individual work of the candidate concerned.

OVERALL TOTAL 600

x 0.058 35

OVERALL TOTAL 240

x 0.175 42

Signature(s) of teacher(s) responsible for the assessment _____

This record card is to be retained until after the publication of results. It is to be made available on request to a moderator.

Reproduced with permission of Northern Partnership for Records of Achievement.

196 Records of progress

The Welsh Joint Education Committee raise another important issue, and follow it with a very reasonable solution:

a   *Skills and abilities relating specifically to one particular module.* Unless these skills and abilities are reinforced in later modules, it is possible that a pupil's attainment in these areas actually declines during the remainder of the course, and that optimum attainment is displayed immediately after the relevant part of the course. In such cases it is acceptable that the assessment is carried out within the one module only.

b   *Skills and abilities developed throughout the course.* It is reasonable to expect that most pupils' attainment in such skills and abilities would be higher at the end of the fifth year compared with what it was, say, twelve months earlier. In order to be fair, therefore, a substantial proportion of the assessment of such skills and abilities should take place towards the end of the whole modular course rather than within individual modular units.[4]

Functional recording keeping

It has been seen how the clarity with which objectives are spelt out, coupled with efficiency of record keeping, can facilitate the construction of individual programmes. When this happens, record keeping becomes functional rather than merely monitorial. It can not only indicate past success or failure but, in the light of this, map out the skills and concepts that need further development. These will include behaviour of an interpersonal nature that the institution wishes to foster, well summarised in Curricular Item 45, from the Northern Partnership for Records of Achievement.

Functional record keeping of this kind takes as its starting point the modular specification (such as that given on page 125), which will incorporate institutional as well as modular objectives. Record cards (Figure 9.1) will need to be completed at the end of each module. On these will be entered the pupil's relative success in each of the fields decided upon, as measured along one of the lines suggested on pages 180–5 above. Then, at the conclusion of each module, this information can be transferred (probably by the pupil's personal tutor) to a centrally-held record sheet.

These recored sheets show the cumulative effect upon an individual's development of all the modules selected. Future modules may be chosen not only to enhance his chances of academic success or to develop certain interests, but also to strengthen areas of weakness, build up skills which

---

[4]   Welsh Joint Education Committee *Guidelines for the Use of Modular Schemes of Assessment,* 1985, p.3.

CURRICULAR ITEM 45
Interpersonal skills in modular group work

Checklist for skills demonstrated during group work

In *planning the activity* the student has demonstrated the ability to:–
contribute to group discussion
listen to others
tolerate others' ideas
accept group decisions
accept the organisation of others
encourage the ideas of others
explain ideas clearly
prioritise tasks
initiate ideas
organise others
question ideas
compromise
In *carrying out group activity*, the student has demonstrated the ability to:–
cooperate
accept a given task
accept the organisation of others
accept others' needs
complete the designated task
a) by perseverence
b) by seeking help
c) by an alternative strategy
d) by accepting help
work without close adult supervision
organise others

Reproduced with permission from *Rules and Guidance* p.16 of Unit Accreditation (Interim Scheme 1) 1985, NPRA.

have been shown to be lacking, or facilitate the development of behaviours which the institution regards as important. It may be, for instance, that oral communication requires more work, that the bases of mathematical computation are missing, that so far the individual has shown himself

---

Figure 9.1

NAME ....   MODULE ....

STAFF ....   DATES ....to ....

CONTENT ....

....

CONCEPTS	SKILLS	BEHAVIOURS
1.	a.	i
2.	b.	ii
3.	c.	iii
4.	d.	iv

---

incapable of working with others or that he is lacking in confidence. Each of these requires developing in a different way and certain modules may contain elements that ensure just the appropriate training will take place. Functional record keeping allows this to happen while still preserving the autonomy of individual choice.

Modifying the modules

Close and positive monitoring of this kind places a good deal of evidence into the hands of those planning each scheme. Alongside the record cards for each individual unit are comments from those who have taught it, those who have acted in a tutorial capacity and – in many cases – the pupils themselves. From this mass of evidence, possibly after a module has run two or three times, various deductions can be made:

- *Module well taken up and received* Look closely at the individual ratings of elements within it, for reasons given below
- *Module unpopular* Consider here how well it fits in with units in the scheme, and comments on the teaching style, and look at individual ratings once more
- *Most pupils perform badly* in all ratings but *comment favourably* on teaching style. Possibly insufficient academic rigour; course badly planned?
- *Most pupils perform badly in some ratings* Strengthen these
- *Most pupils perform well in some ratings* Build on these when restructuring
- *Most pupils perform well overall* This could be good, but consider whether the unit is not too superficial.

And the model . . .

The modular transverse can now be further adapted, as Figure 9.2 shows.

Figure 9.2

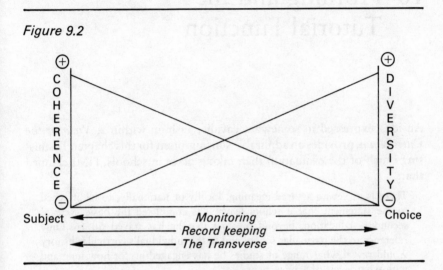

For further reading

Most Examination Boards have now come out with statements regarding the place of modules in GCSE and other examinations: *Guide to Syllabus Developers Proposing Modular Schemes* (East Anglian Examinations Boards, 1985), *A Modular Curriculum, Guidelines for Development* (Midlands Examining Group, 1985), *Guidelines for the Development and Assessment of Modular GCE Examinations* (Northern Examining Associations, 1985), *Guidelines for the Use of Modular Schemes of Assessment* (Welsh Joint Education Committee, Examinations Department, 1985), *Guidelines for the Preparation and Submission of Modular or Unit Based Curriculum Schemes* (Southern Examining Group, 1986), *The Modular Curriculum – a Discussion Document* (Southern Examining Group, 1986) and *Supporting Modular Curriculum Development* (BTEC, 1985).

Of especial interest here is *Evaluation of a Modular Curriculum* by S Pyart (Ysgol Emrys ap Iwan, 1986).

10 Profiling and the Tutorial Function

An idea expressed in somewhat cavalier fashion within *A View of the Curriculum*, provides an admirable starting-point for this chapter. Dismissing much of the evaluation then taking place in schools, HMI claimed that:

> There is as yet no assured meaning, locally or nationally, to be attached to the statement that a school leaver has completed the basic cycle of secondary education, beyond the fact that he has stayed till 16. Only reference to the particular school and to the individual's curricular history would reveal what range of studies he has engaged in, for how long and with what levels of achievement.[1]

Criticism such as this led to the overhaul of the examination system, culminating in GCSE, but elsewhere the remarks were taken in a literal fashion and used positively in a number of ways.

Positive assessment

The GCSE, comprehensive and efficient though it is, cannot possibly measure all aspects of what is achieved through five years of secondary education, nor will every pupil be entered for this examination. The belief that all leavers, regardless of background, destination or ability, should take with them some positive record of everything they have accomplished, be it of an academic, social, or personal nature, underlies many current developments in our schools.

The tutor's or the form teacher's report will give some inkling of this, with its references to clubs and societies joined, participation in dramatic, sporting or musical events, contribution to the running of the institution through prefectorial duties, responsibility for the tuckshop, helping with discos, and care for others exemplified by visits to old people's homes, collecting for charity, assistance with the local crêche, etc . . . But such reports contain no input from the pupil and the amount of consultation

---

[1] HMI *A View of the Curriculum*, HMSO, 1980, p.14.

that takes place before, during and after their compilation varies from school to school.

One way of ensuring that such information is made available to the school is the development of a personal portfolio by each pupil. Curricular Item 46 offers a first-rate example of this, supplied by Parliament Hill School, London.

CURRICULAR ITEM 46
Portfolio, Parliament Hill School, London

This is a list of things to do with school which you could put in your portfolio.

Try to put in evidence connected with as many different things as possible. Put a tick on one of the lines below as you put something in – it will show you how your portfolio is building up and where the 'gaps' might be. Remember – your portfolio doesn't have to include everything listed below, but it will be better if it does!

Subject evidence:

English _____

Mathematics _____

Option A _____

B _____

C _____

D _____

E _____

Others _____

4th/5th Year Timetable

Assessments or Reports

Certificates, Awards, Commendations

School Trips/Fieldwork

Work Experience/Community Work

School Play/Music Group/Club

CURRICULAR ITEM 46 (continued)

Work for Year or School Council

Anything else?

You should include in your portfolio anything you do out of school which is particularly interesting or worthwhile, or which tells other people something about you.

You might spend a lot of time doing one or several of the things on the list below. If so, you've gained experience and skills which could be very useful for you or an employer. Don't keep it to yourself! Include in your portfolio some evidence – it might be a letter, a reference or a photograph.

Remember, this list is only a guide. You can put in your portfolio evidence about anything at all.

CLUBS AND SOCIETIES
Member of any club or society.
Any special responsibility in a club or society.
Organised a newsletter or magazine.
Organised a speaker or a special event.
Acted or helped in a play.

SPORTS
Play any sport regularly.
Play in a sports team.
Organise a sports team.

SPECIAL INTERESTS OR ABILITIES
Craft hobbies, kit building, knitting etc.
Repairing bikes, clothes etc.
Learning or playing musical instruments.
Using home computers.
Using film, video or sound recording equipment.
Taking photographs.
Drawing, painting etc.
Reading.
Babysitting.

CURRICULAR ITEM 46 (continued)

PERSONAL ACHIEVEMENTS

Spoken in front of a large group of people.
Saved up for something special over
a long period of time.
Been on an adventure style of holiday.
Had a letter, article, drawing, painting, poem published.
Served as a guide for a visitor to London.

HELPING FRIENDS OR OTHERS IN THE COMMUNITY

Any work fund raising, sponsored events etc.
Organising a competition or event for charity.
Been on a first aid course.
Learnt to life save.
Helped someone in an accident, called the
emergency services.
Taught someone a special skill, e.g. riding a bike,
wallpapering.
Helped a handicapped or elderly person regularly.
Helped solve a problem between friends,
helped someone get advice.
Looked after someone through an illness.

HOME & GARDEN

Regularly looked after younger brothers or sisters.
Built any simple furniture, put up shelves etc.
Done any decorating, painting or wallpapering.
Done any electrical repairs in the home, changed plugs.
Made any kind of clothes.
Responsible on a regular basis for house cleaning,
laundry, shopping, cooking etc.
Cooked food for a special occasion.
Regularly helped with the garden.
Grown houseplants, plants from seed etc.
Taken regular care of a pet, possibly a sick pet.

EXPERIENCE OF WORK

Any work experience at all.
Any 'promotions' or special achievements.

Recording achievement

The portfolio, detailed above, is one solution to this problem. Another is to produce certificates of educational achievement, such as those currently being developed for school leavers in different parts of the country following the DES *Policy Statements* of 1984 and 1986. Pilot Schemes have now been established in Dorset, the East Midlands, Essex, ILEA, Lancashire, Suffolk, Wigan, Wales and with the OCEA Consortium (Coventry, Leicestershire, Oxfordshire and Somerset) concentrating on four aspects:

- The recognition of achievement
- Motivation and personal development
- Curriculum and organisation
- The 'document of record'[2]

The last-mentioned of the nine pilot schemes is OCEA, which is producing a certificate with three components:

> The *P-Component* provides a means whereby students can reflect on and record the whole range of their learning and development within and beyond the curriculum. The *G-Component* recognises achievement within certain curriculum areas ... The *E-Component* provides a means whereby nationally/publicly recognised qualifications ... can be recorded.[3]

Curricular Item 47 illustrates how closely the student is drawn into this process.

Profiling

The process of building up such a personal record of achievement, or the construction of a profile, is fundamental to most of the ideas of modular planning explored in the last few chapters. Many schools adopting the OCEA approach have, in fact, linked this closely to such schemes.

The profile is usually a single document drawn up over a period of time by the student, with the assistance of a designated member of the teaching staff. This might be a summative statement, like the portfolio, of all that has been achieved, but there is also a strong formative or contractual element involved in arriving at this point. Profiling within modular schemes usually entails 'goal setting based on mutual consent'.[4] Here the tutor's role is of paramount importance, with all the elements noted on pages 207–211 coming into play.

---

[2]   DES *Records of Achievement: a Statement of Policy.* HMSO, 1986, para 11.
[3]   Provisional OCEA Handbook, 1985, p2.
[4]   White, R., Pring, R., Brockington, D. *The 14–18 Curriculum: Integrating CPVE, YTS, TVEI?* Youth Education Services, 1985, p22.

CURRICULAR ITEM 47
The 'P' Component in OCEA Profiling

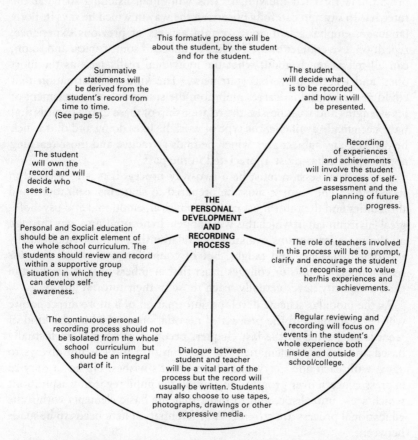

This formative process will be about the student, by the student and for the student.

Summative statements will be derived from the student's record from time to time. (See page 5)

The student will decide what is to be recorded and how it will be presented.

The student will own the record and will decide who sees it.

Recording of experiences and achievements will involve the student in a process of self-assessment and the planning of future progress.

Personal and Social education should be an explicit element of the whole school curriculum. The students should review and record within a supportive group situation in which they can develop self-awareness.

THE PERSONAL DEVELOPMENT AND RECORDING PROCESS

The role of teachers involved in this process will be to prompt, clarify and encourage the student to recognise and to value her/his experiences and achievements.

The continuous personal recording process should not be isolated from the whole school curriculum but should be an integral part of it.

Dialogue between student and teacher will be a vital part of the process but the record will usually be written. Students may also choose to use tapes, photographs, drawings or other expressive media.

Regular reviewing and recording will focus on events in the student's whole experience both inside and outside school/college.

Reproduced with permission from *OCEA Newsletter 5* (January, 1985) University of Oxford Delegacy of Examinations

The tutor's role

The process of profiling commences at the very outset of any programme of work and will involve a completely free exchange of views between the two parties concerned (ie the student and tutor).

To begin with, the member of staff here working in a tutorial capacity will need to have as much information as is available regarding each student's past record. As far as possible these details should be completely open and shared between tutor and tutee. The tutor also needs to be conversant with all the modules that have been prepared and any pre-requisites that have been laid down regarding their interrelationships.

The aim here is not to direct students into specific courses or pre-arranged series of modules, but to discover which is the best possible programme for each individual. This will entail listening to what the tutee has to say and carefully observing the way in which he says it. Body language, emphasis laid upon certain aspects of previous experience, repetition, eye-contact or lack of it, avoidance of some topics, and so on, can all tell as much about what the individual really feels as the most open and lengthy of verbal statements. The kind of information that could prove helpful is: career ambition, the student's own assessment of his strengths and weaknesses, the relationship of these to the records that have been made available, the type of work he likes doing and that which he dislikes, any subject area which he finds attractive and those teaching approaches he has most appreciated in the past.

Any tutorial session must be a two-way process if it is to succeed in its purpose. The student must be prepared to share his aspirations and difficulties and the tutor must create a physical, emotional and psychological environment in which this will happen. In negotiating a way through all the modular options available the relationship is most emphatically *not* that of teacher and taught, but of counsellor and client. For this reason many schools or colleges insist that members of staff working in such a capacity never actually teach those in their tutorial groups.

As the modular scheme develops, information of a more direct nature will be available and the process of negotiation, backed by the kind of records advocated in the last chapter, becomes at once more factually based and more problematic. The function of a tutor is not always to agree with each and every one of his client's wishes. He has a duty to express concern over progress, to caution the pupil regarding aspirations which seem unrealistic, and to insist that the basic elements within the educational process are covered. A differentiation here needs to be made between:

- *directing* an individual into areas for his well-being (but not whole programmes);
- *guiding* him along a path which has been mutually agreed;
- *counselling* certain actions in the light of progress made or future ambitions.

Developing the tutorial role

The FEU have identified four stages in the process of careers guidance and the selection of appropriate training.[5] Within each of these they

---

[5]   Miller, J.C. *Tutoring*. FEU, 1982, pp.9–14

suggest certain skills which need to be developed by the tutor. These could well be 'borrowed', as outlined below, for use within open modular schemes.

Selection of modules

Negotiation with students over the modular choice they should make. This will be based upon the range of factors outlined above and the full use of functional record-keeping.

Contracting – here it becomes important that the tutor really does have full details of the modules that are available and what is required in each. The modular specification, outlined in Chapter 6, is of great importance, as it will indicate in short but precise terms exactly what will be expected of those taking it. If external examinations are involved, then syllabuses need to be available. A contract is, of course, a two-way affair and, whilst those running each module will expect those opting for it to be aware of the commitments involved, the students are entitled to expect a unit to operate according to the ground rules set by its authors.

Liaison with those who are teaching the module over matters arising from the above 'contract'; with those who have previously taught the individual; with the parents, if this is really appropriate; with employers regarding the currency of the unit; and with higher/further education over like matters.

Induction into a module

Advising – regarding the full implications of the approach being adopted and how this matches up to expectations. Advice will also be required regarding study skills, and here an approach analogous to that outlined on pages 171–175 might be taken. If previous advice has not been given, then methods of organising a personal study timetable may be needed.

Monitoring progress through the module, largely by discussion with the student. Problems may be raised by the student but, in any case, should be discovered by the tutor by the kind of questioning referred to in Curricular Item 48. The profile should be kept up to date on such matters, but this should be done openly, with the student's consent.

Counselling on the best way forward should difficulties arise. This needs to be done in the manner most appropriate to the problem being discussed and the individual concerned. Different approaches will be required for different students, but non-verbal communication such as that referred to on page 206 is of great importance here. Counselling may be required over personal matters, poor attendance or lack of progress often being an early indication of this.

Liaising – again, with the teaching staff, but only if such an approach has been agreed by the student. Confidentiality of information is an important bond between tutor and tutee and to break it is to jeopardise the relationship which is at the heart of the counselling process. If information must be shared with others, the student should always be informed.

Experience within module

Confronting – A tutor must never be afraid to face a student with evidence of misdemeanour or poor progress. Openness is not merely a cosy chat or a pooling of platitudes. It is an adult two-way process in which honesty is the key to success. Naturally, a confrontational encounter needs once more to be related to the temperament of the individual concerned and it is vital that the facts are correct and available.

Feeding back of evidence from teaching staff or the results of enquiries made on a student's behalf.

Referring for advice or treatment of a more specialised kind. In academic terms this may be to the Departmental Head, the Admissions Tutor in Higher Education or the librarian. Vocational modules may need the active support of industry. In some cases consultation or treatment of a medical or psychiatric nature may be required. A tutor must, above all, not regard himself as a fully trained medic or psychologist. Yet, at the same time, he must recognise the early signs of, say, mental breakdown, drug abuse, etc. It is then a case of referring the student to the correct quarter. Regular INSET provision on early-warning signals of breakdowns such as those alluded to above is therefore of great importance.

Transition between modules

Assessing progress made in the last module against past records plotted on the module chart, and discussing the outcomes with each student. How far the tutorial role needs to be divorced from that of active curricular assessment is still a matter of some contention.

Evaluating the best module to choose as a follow-up, in a developmental sequence. Should plans discussed at an earlier stage be continued, or should there be some branching within the programme at this stage?

Counselling As a result of this, or rather in consultation with the student, advice needs to be given and the policy talked through, including the full implications of any course of action.

Referring once again, for more detailed advice.

Central to the whole process is the interview between tutor and tutee, in which an on-going profile is built up. The structuring of these meetings and the use of questions to obtain the requisite information therefore needs consideration. Curricular Item 48 is from a managerial context, but indicates exactly what might be achieved in this way:

CURRICULAR ITEM 48
The Use of Questions

Questioning

The most obvious of the skills needed here is that of being able to ask the right question at the right moment in the right way. Generalisation is difficult, but the following types of questions might prove helpful:

Type of Question	Example	Usage
Open	How do you find Class 1b as a group?	Such questions cannot be answered merely in the negative or the affirmative; they require the interviewee to be expansive, to give some further information. Such responses could be factual, or relate to emotions, attitudes or preconceptions. Questions prefaced with the words *Why, Where, What, When* or *How* are impossible to answer with a Yes or a No. The individual has to be more forthcoming.
Closed	From what you say you seem to find the younger classes more of a problem. Am I right?	Such questions permit no expansion. Although the approach may be somewhat negative, they may be useful in giving the interviewee confidence by repeating back what has been said, for ensuring that you are both on the same track or summarising the position before moving on to the next point.
Specific	Have you discussed this with Mr O'Connor?	This type of question requires specific information. There can only be one correct or truthful answer and, naturally, such questions are helpful for getting at precise information that you want or pinning down an individual who tends to go off at an angle or to 'waffle'.

CURRICULAR ITEM 48 (continued)

Type of Question	Example	Usage
Reflective	J: 'No-one seems to realise. Things are so difficult at home.' S: 'I am sorry things are that bad. At home you say?'	Here a statement is rephrased or repeated, and handed back to the interviewee. This indicates continued interest, stops him from going off on to another point too soon and avoids personal involvement or bias.
Reverse	J: 'Whatever am I going to do about my husband's attitude? Should I leave him, put up with it, or leave my job?' S: 'What do you think you should do, Jenny?'	Similar to the *reflective* question in that no 'side' is being taken and the problem is passed back to the interviewee. Here, though, the idea is not to reach facile solutions too soon; but to help the teacher think through the various courses of action.
Leading	Don't you really feel that you should seek some more specialised advice?	This is the rhetorical question transferred to the privacy of the interview room. Only one answer is really required. If handled badly all the interviewer receives is reinforcement of his own ideas; he learns nothing about the interviewee. However, it can be a good test of attitudes, prejudices, or possibilities. It is a type of question that could well evoke an emotive response.
Hypothetical	Supposing I was to lighten your teaching load a little? How would you use the additional time?	This does not committ the interviewer to a course of action, but explores possibilities only. It asks for a constructive contribution from the interviewee, testing his ability to deal with a problem and come to grips with a possible solution. Very helpful, such questions, in assisting the interviewer to reach a conclusion, especially at selection interviews.

It is not suggested that the full range of questions should be used in every interview, nor that the order above should slavishly be

CURRICULAR ITEM 48 (continued)

followed. Questions serve precisely the function of the steering wheel, accelerator and gear lever in a car – they adjust the speed of the exchange, ensure that it is heading in the right direction and modulate the ratio between power input (interviewer) and output (interviewee).

Reproduced with permission from D.W. Warwick: *Interviews & Interviewing*, Industrial Society, 1984.

Making use of the profile

Profiling represents a large investment of time and energy, but if completed in the manner suggested above it is clearly worth the effort in terms of student motivation, the reputation of the school or college as a genuinely 'caring' establishment and the recognition given by employers to such schemes.

The purpose for which the profile will be used largely determines its content, format and the style with which it is written. It may be:

a For the *student's* benefit – as a personal record of his schooling, to be used largely as a keepsake or memento. Here, the format can be fairly flexible. It will need to be well presented, as a tangible sign that individual worth is recognised. A photograph could be included, along with those of his friends, and space provided for autographs, etc. All this should not be dismissed as sentimentality. If the institution has been the kind of place it ought to be, any pupil would wish to have such a memento of the five most formative years of his life.

b For the *employer* The individual's own comments here need to be placed alongside those of his teachers, tutor and Head/Principal. Some character reference is required as well as a full record of academic and personal achievement. All this should be presented in a positive manner, the golden rule being – 'If you can't think of anything good to say, write nothing'!

c For the *school* Here the kind of record-keeping outlined on pages 196–8 will be of central interest, both in the assessment of modular courses and, for the writing of references after the individual has left. The profile is, of course, also used by schools as a formative kind of assessment in negotiating programmes of work.

Documentation

Modular schemes can generate rather a lot of paper, especially if external assessment of any kind is involved. What begins as a proper concern for clear record-keeping, good two-way communication and open access to information, can eventually reach proportions which threaten to obscure the raison d'être of the scheme. As much time can be spent on the completion of forms as is devoted to the planning and teaching of the modules themselves!

Clearly, some central policy has to be devised from an early stage to prevent this happening, and those that are working within the scheme need to be closely involved in decisions that are taken. It is better for time to be spent at the very beginning in discussing such matters and taking appropriate action than to have to respond to each problem as it arises, with each department taking unilateral decisions regarding such issues. Of course, the policy, once outlined, will need up-dating and modification as the scheme develops, in precisely the way suggested by the specification sheet given on page 125. All such changes, however, should be made in the light of the central principles involved. The major questions to be discussed are:

- What are the different kinds of documents to be produced?
- What precise purpose does each serve?
- Is there any duplication between them?
- Who are they for?
- By whom will they be completed?
- How 'open' is the information they contain?
- Where will they be stored?
- For how long will they be kept?

As far as possible, a school needs to standardise its forms so that, across the curriculum and within each year, the teacher knows precisely what is required of him and is not faced with having to supply the same information on several occasions in different ways. At the same time, differentiation can be achieved between sections of the school – years, houses, departments, faculties etc – through a system of colour-coding. All Chemistry documents might be in red, History ones in blue, German in yellow, and so on. A differentiation might be made between the different documents – modular specifications, banked modules, record cards etc – in this way, if it was felt more appropriate. See, for example, the standardisation of documents at Hemsworth High School (page 135) and Thomas Tallis (page 131).

Comment banking and computers

A further consideration relates to the storage of these documents, the length of time they need to be kept and their confidentiality. Two rather controversial issues are the use of comment banking and computers in record-keeping and reference-writing.

Comment banking is being developed nationally in relation to CPVE. The 'bank' consists of a full range of carefully-graded comments, which can be called up and entered onto a form. Some maintain that this not only saves the teacher a vast amount of time – in dealing with a large number of comments and preparing a document containing them – but may also supply him with comments that he might not have considered. The objections, of course, are that this depersonalises the whole situation, and that the very ease of comment banking could detract from the tutorial function. It has already been noted (on page 103) that any school with a well developed computer section is at an advantage in the running of such schemes. Here, the main objections are the possible lack of confidentiality over comments and information and, again, the depersonalising effect of the microprocessor.

Modifying the model

A final modification may now be made to the central model running throughout this text, based on the amount of tutorial input invested in such a scheme and the nature of this involvement. More formal approaches to the left of the transverse permit little freedom of choice; it is merely a matter of providing the correct sequence of modules and ensuring that pupils get the most from them. The tutorial function is little in evidence here.

As one moves to the right, so the amount of choice allowed increases and, with it, the need for supervision. Control is sometimes vested in a pre-structuring of modules but, if not, then the tutor's role becomes rather more specialised and is of greater importance.

On page 206 it was suggested that *direction, guidance* and *counselling* were three elements within the tutorial role. Each will tend to come to the fore at different stages along the transverse, as the balance switches progressively from one curricular extreme to the other. The pattern, then, will tend to look like that in Figure 10.1.

Figure 10.1

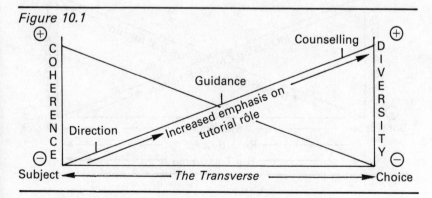

Conclusion

Versatility has been identified as the key feature of the module throughout this book. Its brevity and the need to make objectives quite explicit combine to bring the internal components into a dynamic, rather than a static, relationship. In other words, a fair degree of negotiation is possible between the *teacher* and the *pupils* over the nature of the *material* they will be following and how it might be tackled. This enables the *module* to form the basis of a large number of curricular patterns.

Two extremes that have been cited are: the *course* – in which subject material is rigorously analysed and broken down into a clear progression of sub-units, the content and order of which is shared with the pupils; and the *scheme* – in which individuals are permitted to create their own on-going synthesis through the selection of modules from a variety of sources. The former is strong on coherence but balances the possibility of teacher domination through an emphasis upon clarity of aims and direction. The latter, which could lead to epistemological fragmentation, usually offsets this through tutorial guidance, the careful monitoring of progress or some pre-structuring of the material.

Similarly, the balance between *formative* (unit credits) and *summative* (terminal examination) *assessment* is often achieved through a system of portfolios, profiles, records of achievement or differential weighting between various elements of the course.

To get the best out of modular planning, then, a series of checks and balances has to be brought into play between all the elements mentioned above and described in this book. The completed version of the *model* which has been built up throughout illustrates this (Figure 10.2).

Figure 10.2

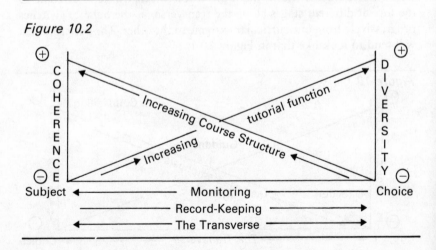

From such a basis, a large number of curricular structures may be derived, of which the following are but a few. Although it is suggested that each is appropriate to certain levels within the system, individual elements are transposable between them.

Primary
Here the problem is that set out on page 40, the need for greater specialist input in a generalist organisation. Certain teachers are here designated as being responsible for specific subject areas (see DES list page 40). They prepare short, say, three-week modules together with the class teacher, coming in either at the outset to give a 'lead lesson' with him or at some other appropriate stage. This work is then followed up, with regular meetings taking place between specialist and classroom teacher(s) in order to monitor progress. The specialist's class is taken by a teacher with whom he is regularly working, to facilitate occasional, more specific, treatment of a topic, or in team-teaching situations this can be accommodated across the staff.

Some of the various organisational patterns possible are indicated below (Figure 10.3).

Primary

Figure 10.3

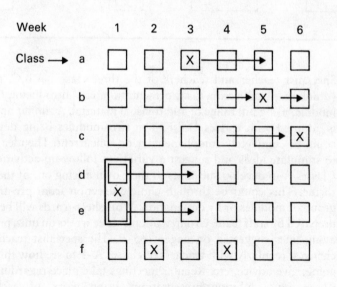

X = Specialist input

Primary/Middle

Figure 10.4

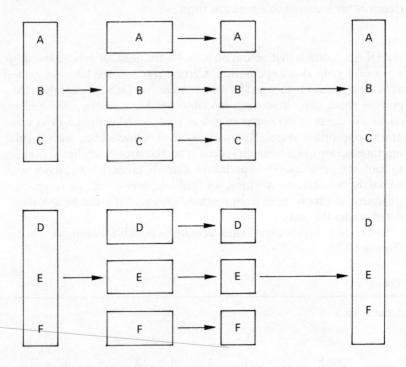

1   Specialist teacher and teachers of the three classes A,B,C, prepare stimulating lead lesson, visit, presentation, etc, introducing topic of module, using full range of audio-visual material. A similar approach is adopted with classes D,E,F. The two modules being developed could be completely complementary or concurrent. The idea here is to stimulate ideas and suggest a variety of follow-up activities.

2   Classes A–F develop sub-units of their own arising out of the major theme. This could be through choice, selection from pre-arranged group of modules or by designation. Worksheets/cards will be jointly prepared by staff team. Group work for three weeks on unit, probably along lines suggested on pages 165–9. The specialist teacher 'exchanges' regularly with teachers of classes A–F to see how things are going, give advice, etc. Regular meetings take place regarding this.

3   Classroom exhibitions/presentations bring work of each unit together.

4   Large exhibition/display/presentation allows pupils to learn from one another's work and for teachers to evaluate scheme.

Lower Secondary

Figure 10.5

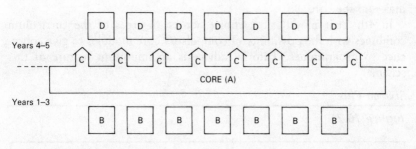

A The pupils' experiences are shaped in Years 1–3 by a subject-based core, possibly consisting of elements suggested by HMI in *Curriculum 11–16* (see page 41).

B The 'essential elements' referred to on page 47 and study skills are supplied by compulsory modules, prepared by teams of staff on a cross-disciplinary basis.

C In Year 4 modular options are available within subject/faculty divisions.

D Compulsory modules ensure continuation of core by linking all these areas and developing areas of self-directed learning.

Secondary

Figure 10.6

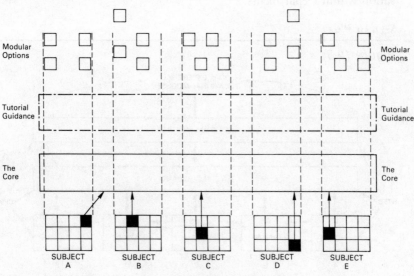

Modules are developed within each major subject area, which also supplies a module(s) explaining how their work relates to what else is going on. These, together with subject-generated modules on study skills, make up the core.

In 4th Year modular/free/choice across all areas of the curriculum combines with the possibility of compulsory core modules to give coherence to programmes. Tutorial advice is an important feature of this scheme.

Sixteen Plus

Figure 10.7

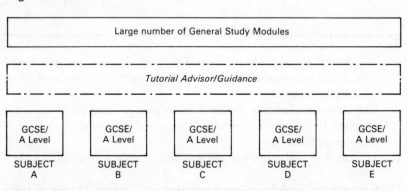

A level/GCSEs are taken within subject areas. A large range of General Study modules complement, develop, bridge and extend these areas. Non-examination programmes are also built up, with possibly some modularisation within Departments.

Sixteen Plus

Figure 10.8

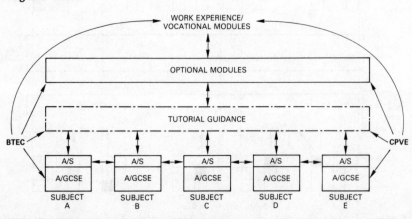

The addition of A/S Level work and modules of a vocational nature makes the whole system more 'open', with modules being selected from all areas of the curriculum, and the building up of a profile and strong tutorial support.

For further reading

The key documents regarding Records of Achievement are: *Records of Achievement: a Statement of Policy* (DES, 1984) and the 1986 *Policy Statement*. The various pilot schemes mentioned in the text all produce outlines of their work.

Three recent publications on profiling are: *Records of Achievement at Sixteen* by T Burgess and E Adams (NFER/Nelson, 1985), *Profiles and Records of Achievement* by R Broadfoot (Holt, Rinehart and Winston, 1985) and *Profiles and Profiling Procedures* by G Hitchcock (Longman, 1985).

Welfare systems within schools are dealt with by P Laing and M Marland (eds) in *New Directions in Pastoral Care* (Basil Blackwell, 1985), by P Ribbins *et al* in *Schooling and Welfare* (Falmer Press, 1985), by J Raymond in *Implementing Pastoral Care in Schools* (Croom Helm, 1985) and by D Hamblin in *Problems and Practice in Pastoral Care* (Basil Blackwell, 1981).

The management of such systems is the theme of *Head of House, Head of Year* by K Blackburn (Heinemann, 1983) and *Leading a Pastoral Team* by L Bell and P Maher (Basil Blackwell, 1986). The role of the tutor is covered in J C Miller's *The Tutor* (FEU, 1982) and in *Guidance 16–19* by D Hamblin (Basil Blackwell, 1983).

Index

inter departmental 12, 14, 46, 88
teacher/pupil 6
Reports
 Cockcroft 10
 Hargreaves 6, 11, 25, 149
 Plowden 40
 Taylor 65
 writing 80
Research 151, 171
Resources 40, 151, 152, 170, 173

SEB 10
SEC 66
SREB 26, 28, 100
St Kentigern's Academy 67–71
Scottish Action Plan 126
School
 Council 66
 infant 2, 38, 113
 primary 39–41, 113, 215, 216
 secondary 41, 53
 visits 11
Science 13, 26, 40, 41, 43, 45, 50, 54, 64,
  88, 91, 192–6
Science & technology 28, 60, 142
Self-supported study 185
Seventeen Plus 28
Simulation 151, 159
Sixth form 48, 55, 85, 170–1
Skills 48, 115, 180, 189
Skinner, B.F. 10
Slides 155
Social abilities 40
Social studies 13, 50, 182
Sociology 50, 160
Spanish 19
Staff development 15–16
Stenhouse, L. 152
Streaming 10
Study skills 19, 47–9, 155, 173, 207, 217,
 218
Subject
 department 12, 42–3, 49, 83, 134, 165,
  174, 175, 218
 faculty 43–6, 85, 101, 165
 integration 14, 88

TEC 78
TVEI 1, 11, 12, 13, 62, 65, 72–7, 92, 93,
 97, 126, 128–30, 172

Taster units 12, 72, 97
Teachers 40, 173
 dominant 20, 214
 role 26, 168–9
 team 45, 94, 102, 165–9, 215
 training 40
Teaching machines 70
Teaching Quality 40
Team 12, 40, 44, 45, 102, 165–9, 215, 216
Technical drawing 13, 19
Technology 61, 64, 181
Tests 20, 178
Textiles 51, 62
Themes 72, 88–90, 160, 166, 175
Thomas Tallis School 147–8, 179, 181–3,
 186, 212
Thorn EMI 78–80
Timetable 2, 12, 53, 66, 100–1, 142, 162,
 171, 172
Time, Place & Society Project 43, 85
Topics 40, 166, 173–6
 choice 171
 sheet 174
Tutor
 personal 49, 62, 134, 172, 200
 subject 142
 role 171, 205–11
 referral 208
Tutorial work 33, 47, 171–176, 206, 213,
 217, 219

View of the Curriculum, A 180, 200
Videos 66, 151, 155
Visits 11, 155
Vocational work 78, 219

Watson 10
Wantage School 50–3
Warwick, D. 81, 169, 211
Welsh Joint Education Committee 196
White Paper 66
World of work 15, 47
Work cards 41, 151, 155, 216
Work experience 11, 203, 218
Work sheets 41, 155, 216
Written comments 185

YTS 1
Ysgol Emrys ap Iwan 26, 29, 30, 53–5, 142–
 44, 145–7, 148, 162